The
Cleis Press
Sextionary

The
Cleis Press
Sextionary

From the
Editors of Cleis Press

CLEiS
PRESS

Published in the United States by Cleis Press, an imprint of Start Midnight, LLC, 101 Hudson Street, Thirty-Seventh Floor, Suite 3705, Jersey City, NJ 07302.

Printed in the United States.
Cover design: Scott Idleman/Blink
Cover illustration: Time Tunnel
Text design: Frank Wiedemann
First Edition.
10 9 8 7 6 5 4 3 2 1

Trade paper ISBN: 978-1-62778-230-2
E-book ISBN: 978-1-62778-231-9

Library of Congress Cataloging-in-Publication Data is available on file.

INTRODUCTION

Home base. The final frontier. Gettin' it on. Doing it. There are so many phrases and euphemisms to describe the act of sex. But what *is* sex? Is it an act of love, or lust? One of procreation? One of power? Few people define sex the same exact way; some define it strictly as the physical side, others as the emotional, but far more have the view that it's something in between, a combination of perfect mind and body gratification.

What we can say for sure is that sex is a driving factor for almost every human being, and just as with the other things that drive our daily lives (eating, traveling, vying for control), there are millions of ways to experience it. This book is here to help you understand those myriad *how*s in the realm of sex. From sex positions to fetishes to the many existing sexual identities, we'll explore just what it means to be a sexual creature on this earth.

Notes and terms to know before using the Sextionary

Sex
For the purposes of this book, we will use the following definition: Sex is an act where one, two, or more people stimu-

late themselves or each other in a way that is extremely pleasurable for at least one of the parties. This can trigger a physical release called an **orgasm** (see page 107).

Genitals

While medical usage focuses solely on the parts that are used for reproduction, in this book, the word *genitals* refers to the areas and parts of the body which are most often the focus of sexual satisfaction. These include the vagina, clitoris, labia, penis, testicles, scrotum, and anus.

Consent

Consent is confirmation (written or oral) that someone is willing to perform a specific sexual activity. It is advised to get consent from any new sexual partner and before any new sexual act performed, even with an established partner.

Nonconsensual Activities

Before moving on, we'd like to focus on the "pleasurable for at least one of the parties" part of the sex definition. While we recognize that pain can be pleasurable for some, and that partners may be willing to harm one another to achieve sexual release, we do not want to encourage any nonconsensual activity, i.e., causing pain that isn't specifically requested or having sex against their partner's will. Terms involving nonconsensual activities are listed in a separate part of the book (see Nonconsensual terms, page 233).

We recognize that these terms and acts are part of the sexual lexicon, but we do not condone them and do not encourage readers of the *Sextionary* to participate in any of these listed sexual acts.

Foreplay

This refers to any act that is meant to initiate sexual response in oneself or a partner. It's the act that gets things started, and people's preferences for foreplay vary as much as their preferences for sex. For some people, kissing alone can trigger desire, and for others it could be a look of intense longing or a few words. A lot of people like multiple kinds of foreplay, including touching, licking, or even dancing.

Penetrative Sex

Also known as **intercourse**, penetrative sex is any sex act where a part of the body, such as a penis or finger, or an object, such as a sex toy, is inserted into an orifice of the body, such as a vagina, mouth, or anus. This includes the "typical" (often religious) definition of sex; namely, penis-in-vagina sex, which is a natural form of procreation.

The opposite of this is **outercourse**, where sexual stimulation happens outside of the body, by rubbing partners' body parts against one another or onto something else.

For the penetrative sex positions listed in this book, the terms **giving partner** and **receiving partner** will be used. The **giving partner** is the one doing the penetrating. The

receiving partner is the one being penetrated, either vaginally or anally.

Oral Sex

Oral sex is any sex act where a body part or an object is inserted into or makes contact with the mouth. There are as many euphemisms for oral sex as there are for sex, and you'll find many of them listed in this *Sextionary*.

For the oral sex positions listed in this book, the **giving partner** is the one using their mouth, and the **receiving partner** is the one who is having a part of their body stimulated by their partner's mouth.

Gender and Sexuality

The world of genders is as expansive as the world of sex, and still growing. However, while gender and sexuality can definitely be related, they are entirely different entities. **Gender** is a state of personal being and identity. It's a part of *who you are as a person*, whether male, female, cisgender (identifying as the gender that corresponds with the one you were assigned at birth), transgender (not identifying with your birth-assigned gender), nonbinary, or something completely different. **Sexuality** is something you *experience or have*. For example, a gay man is someone who identifies as male and who experiences sexual attraction to other men; but he is also more than his attraction to men. It's not who he is; it's the way he experiences sexual feeling.

It can be a little confusing, because in today's world there are many people who identify with their sexuality as much as with their gender, but this strong sense of identity tends to come from confrontation and oppression from outside forces. If you ask most "straight" (heterosexual) people who they are, they will not respond with "I am a straight person"; they will likely say "I am a man/woman/ person" or describe their career, race, or nationality, because heterosexuality is still considered the "neutral" state of sexual being. Heterosexuals do not have to fear punishment or cultural shame for their sexual orientation. Since most everything besides male/female heterosexuality is still constantly attacked by those who think it is wrong or immoral, some people are taking a stand for their sexual freedom by including their sexuality in their identity. There is so much more to talk about in terms of identity, but that's a whole other book.

We will not be talking about gender identity in the *Sextionary*, choosing instead to focus on sexuality and sex acts. Some sex acts and fetishes are gender-specific, and that is noted; if a fetish or sex act involves a specific gender identity that may not be widely known, that gender identity will be defined. Also, we will be using the gender-neutral pronouns "they/them/their" throughout this book, as any gender should be able to participate in these sex acts.

BDSM and Kink
BDSM stands for Bondage, Domination, Sadism, and

Masochism. This is the term for sex acts or sexual lifestyles that involve erotic exchanges of power. This exchange takes many forms, but typically includes one (or more) partner who is in charge, also known as the **Dominant** partner, and one (or more) partner who follows the Dominant partner's orders, known as the **Submissive**. The Dominant/Submissive relationship, also called **Master/Slave** relationship, is a partnership built on extreme trust and communication. It does not necessarily involve extremely painful activities, but when it does, participants are referred to as **sadists**, those who experience pleasure by inflicting pain on others, and **masochists**, those who experience pleasure by having pain inflicted upon them.

"BDSM" and "kink" are often used interchangeably, though kink is a more general term for anything that someone personally considers unusual in the realm of sex. For example, many people would say that sex outside is kinky, but for people who prefer or typically have sex outside, it's not kinky at all.

Sexual Preference and Fetishes

A good portion of this *Sextionary* discusses the different kinds of fetishes that exist in the world. A **fetish** is an involuntary sexual obsession with an object or act. People with fetishes experience intense sexual arousal when viewing or experiencing the things they like. Fetishes have fascinated us for centuries, but we're still not quite sure why they develop. Some of them, like adult breastfeeding (see page 9), must surely develop in childhood, but others, like glove fetishes (see page 71), can come out of nowhere and at any time in life. Sexologists (those who study human sexual interests) are still trying to figure out why some fetishes develop, and why they tend to last a lifetime once they do.

Sexual preferences are like fetishes in that they trigger sexual responses in people. However, they are not obsessions. The difference is nominal, but clear: someone with a glove fetish will always choose a partner wearing gloves over a partner who isn't, while someone with a sexual preference for gloved partners can have sex with partners who are not wearing gloves and still have a good time. Sexual preferences are sought out by those who experience them, but do not fully drive the sexual response.

Sexual Conditions

Sometimes people have trouble experiencing the physical or mental stimulation that is commonly associated with sex, or have issues that prevent healthy sexual activity. These issues are called **sexual conditions**, though they are also known as sexual dysfunctions. We use the term "condition" here because most of these issues can be resolved through medication, therapy, or other methods, and we do not believe they should be shameful. Sexual conditions can be caused by many things, including stress, age, or injury. They should not prevent anyone from having a fulfilling sexual life. If you believe you have a sexual condition that is hindering your sexual activity, consult your doctor or a sex therapist.

The Sextionary

24/7 slavery
A type of BDSM relationship in which one person takes on an intense and continuous submissive role. The submissive person gives complete control of the relationship over to the master (the dominant person) in every aspect of life, and agrees to complete any and all of the master's demands. This is different from other BDSM relationships in which the submissive gives up control only during sex or scheduled BDSM events.

A

A-frame
A piece of BDSM/domination furniture that is used to bind and whip submissive participants. Typically made of wood or metal, it comprises of two vertical beams joined together at the top and splayed apart at the bottom, forming a triangle shape. There are usually two or more horizontal support beams for the submissive to lean against, which also serve as points to tie up their wrists or ankles. This is similar to the X-frame or St. Andrew's Cross (see page 193).

A-spot
Scientifically known as the anterior fornix erogenous zone, this is an area inside the vagina, typically right above the entrance to the cervix, which can cause extreme arousal and pleasure for some when stimulated.

abasiophilia

A fetish for or attraction to people with impaired mobility, especially those who use mobility assistance devices, like wheelchairs, orthopedic casts, or leg braces. Loss of limb (amputation) isn't a requirement for this attraction (though it is for acrotomophilia—see page 8), as long as the impairment is visible, as a limp or otherwise.

> Although it may seem strange at first glance, humans have been practicing forms of abasiophilia for thousands of years. From foot binding in China to metal neck rings worn by tribes in Burma and Thailand, the limiting of mobility was often used as a form of control or as a symbol of status. Some people even consider a preference for high-heeled shoes to be a light version of abasiophilia, as heels can limit a person's ability to walk.

ABC party

A fetish community gathering where participants must wear "anything but clothes." This can be interpreted as being naked, but it also invites attendees to be creative and to fashion coverings out of things like boxes, tape, or even body paint.

ablutophilia

The experience of sexual arousal from taking a shower or bath. This differs from aquaphilia (see page 21) in that it's not entirely about the water; the acts of cleaning oneself and of rinsing in the water are both equal for this fetish.

absolute power exchange
Abbreviated as APE, this is a completely interdependent relationship between a master and slave, and extends beyond sexual experiences into everyday life (see 24/7 slavery, page 3). In an APE, the slave has given total physical and mental control over to their master for the duration of their relationship. This is also sometimes referred to as *total power exchange*, or TPE.

abstinence
The choice not to partake in some or all types of sexual activity, whether for religious, medical, or other reasons. For some, this means refraining from any form of vaginal, anal, or oral penetration, but does not limit activities such as masturbation.

ace
A nickname or self-referential term for those who are asexual (see asexuality, page 23).

acmegenesis
An old term for orgasm (see page 107) or the full phase of orgasming.

"Acmegenesis" may sound like an evil company from a cartoon, but it's actually derived from the Greek words "acme," meaning "peak" or "at the height of," and "genesis," meaning "creation" or sometimes "starting point" or "beginning." Orgasms have typically been associated with the beginning of life (though we know that orgasms are not necessary for pregnancy to occur) and so the term was used to describe the moment when life begins during conception.

acomoclitic
Someone who likes or prefers hairless genitals, whether on themselves or their partner. Acomoclitics are particularly fond of the experience of shaving a partner (and thus being the one to cause the hairlessness).

acousticophilia
Acousticophiliacs experience sexual arousal from sound. This can include people who are stimulated by specific sounds, such as a certain song, noise, or even a specific language or accent, but it also includes people who love hearing their partners moan or grunt or make other noises during sex.

acrophilia
A love of being in high places or at great altitudes. Those with acrophilia may experience sexual stimulation either from simply being in a high place, or from the thought

or act of intercourse at a location of great height (such as in an airplane or on a mountain). Also see the Mile High Club (page 98).

acrotomophilia
A fetish for amputees or those with shortened limbs. This is a type of abasiophilia (see page 5).

actirasty
The experience of sexual arousal from exposure to sunlight.

acucullophilia
An attraction to or personal preference for uncircumcised penises (penises that have not had the foreskin removed, either through surgery or otherwise).

adolescentilism
A love of being treated like an adolescent during intercourse, or of watching one's partner dress or act as an adolescent. This is also sometimes called "teenism." Adolescentilism is a type of age play (see page 12).

adult baby
Often abbreviated as AB, this is someone who enjoys role-playing as a baby, including things like drinking from a bottle or wearing a diaper. This fetish is also referred to as paraphilic infantilism. This is a type of age play (see page 12).

Communities that cater to adult babies are known as adult baby crèches or adult baby nurseries. These are places where ABs can go to be cared for by trained professionals as if they were babies. There are also many sexual consultants who offer nanny or babysitting services for adult babies.

adult breastfeeding
Also known as lactophilia, this is a fetish for those who love breastfeeding, or sucking on a woman's breast for nourishment. Couples who practice adult breastfeeding sometimes refer to themselves as a "nursing couple" or as being in an adult nursing relationship.

adult buffet
A type of consensual orgy (see page 108) at which every attendee is available for any other attendee to have sex with, much like how you can take whatever you like from a buffet table.

adult toy
The generic name for a toy that can be used for sexual stimulation. This refers to toys that are made specifically for sexual purposes, but can also be used to describe a regular toy that is used during intercourse. These are also called sex toys or erotic toys.

There are many, many types of adult toys—far too many to include in this *Sextionary*. The basic types, such as dildos (see page 50), vibrators (see page 218), butt plugs (see page 35), and cock rings (see page 41), are included. If you are interested in further exploring adult toys, we recommend going to your local adult store and asking for recommendations. Toys can add a whole new level of excitement to your love life, and there is absolutely no shame in using them to achieve stimulation or orgasm. After all, humans have used tools to make their lives better for thousands of years, and sex toys are simply tools of satisfaction.

adultery

The term for when a married person has sex with someone other than the person they are married to, without consent from their married partner. Adultery can cause a violation of trust within the marriage and will often end a marriage.

aftercare

A BDSM term that refers to the period after intercourse when partners tend to each other's physical or emotional needs. Because BDSM often involves acts that can (always consensually) hurt the other person, aftercare is of the utmost importance to make sure that both parties, particularly the submissive, are in a healthy state after things have finished. This is often a time of deep bonding and communication between BDSM couples.

afterglow
The extended feeling of pleasure after a sexual experience. Afterglow can happen after any stage of the sexual experience, though it most often refers to the moments after orgasm.

afternoon delight
A term for having sex in the afternoon, or taking a recess from daily activities like work in order to have sex or participate in sexual activities. Also referred to as a "nooner."

agalmatophilia
Also known as statuephilia or mannequin love, this is the term for a sexual attraction to statues, mannequins, dolls, or other inanimate objects that resemble humans.

There is a growing phenomenon, mostly found in Japan (though it has made its way to the United States and other parts of the world), of people who date, love, and have sex with body pillows that have images of fictional animated characters or celebrities (often pornographic celebrities) on them. Referred to as *dakimakura* in Japanese, or "love pillows" in English, these pillows are often readily available at anime and comic stores in Japan, and in many online stores. The phenomenon is called "2-D love" in reference to the characters printed on the pillow, but because the pillows are physical objects, it does fit into the realm of agalmatophilia.

age of consent
The legal age at which a person can give consent for any type of sexual activity. This age differs by region; in some areas, laws governing the age of consent may not exist at all.

age play
This refers to sexual role-play in which one or more partners pretend to be of a different age. Age play can involve a preference for someone significantly older or younger. Some types of age play include adolescentilism (see page 8) and adult baby play (see adult baby, page 8).

agnosexual
Someone who is undecided about their sexuality, or someone who may have experienced attraction to a certain gender once or a few times but is unsure whether or not he or she has a preference.

agonophilia
1. A tendency to become aroused by (always consensual) pretend sexual violence, such as struggling, fighting, or being forced, or a person who is aroused by seeing their partner struggle or by pretending to force their partner. This is also known as consensual rape or pseudo-rape.

2. A tendency to become aroused by physical fighting, such as boxing or martial arts. This can also extend to objects

that are used during fighting, such as boxing gloves or protective body padding.

Pseudo-rape can be a touchy subject, especially if one person would like to experience it and the other does not want to. **Never** do anything your partner does not consent to, even if you are in a committed relationship or married. If you and your partner want to try an agono-philia scenario, it is suggested that you script the entire scene (write everything down) for your first few times and discuss everything you intend to do before you start, and make sure you practice aftercare (see page 10) when you are done.

---

agoraphilia

1. A fetish for having sex outdoors, such as in meadows, in forests, or on beaches. (Also see ecosexual, page 55).

2. A fetish for sex in public places. Agoraphiliacs are often also exhibitionists (see page 59) who experience arousal at the thought of being caught having sex in a public place.

agrexophilia

A tendency to be turned on by having other people know about one's sexual activities. This is related to exhibitionism (see page 59) in that both involve having people know about one's sexual experiences, but agrexophiliacs do not need a direct audience. They only need to know that others are aware.

algolagnia
The term for receiving sexual pleasure from the experience of physical pain, especially when the pain is inflicted on one's erogenous zones.

allorgasmia
A sexual condition in which a person must think about someone other than their current partner in order to achieve orgasm. It is also referred to as alloandrism when the person fantasized about is a man, or allogynia when the person fantasized about is a woman.

Allorgasmia is a common condition for those who have been with the same partner for a long time. A lot of people find it shameful or classify it as cheating, which can cause strain in a relationship, but it is important to note that this condition is typically caused by a handful of reasons, including boredom with routine and stress caused by regular life events (financial worries, job stress, family stress, etc.). Allorgasmia often goes away with time, but its exit can be hastened by talking with your partner about what might be wrong and working together to fix issues that you have the power to change.

---

allosexual
People who experience sexual arousal of some kind. This term is typically used to differentiate from asexuals (see page 23) or gray asexuals (see page 72).

allotriorasty
A sexual preference for those who are a different race or ethnicity from oneself.

alpha sub
The name for the submissive with the most power, or who is in the highest hierarchical position in a polyamorous Master/slave relationship with multiple slaves. Also referred to as the senior slave. (Also see Master, page 97, and slave, page 182).

altocalciphilia
A fetish or sexual preference for high-heeled shoes. Arousal may be experienced by wearing high heels, by seeing them on another person, or by simply interacting with high heels in some way. See the note about abasiophilia on page 5. Also related to foot fetishes (see page 65).

alvinolagnia
A sexual fetish for another person's stomach.

amaurophilia

1. A sexual preference or fetish for blind people, being blind, or experiencing sex in places with no visible light.

2. A preference or fetish for not being seen, or not being fully seen, during sex. This can include a range of activities, from having sex with the lights off to using a glory hole (see page 70).

anaclitism

A sexual preference for things one was exposed to as an infant. This could include things like toys, songs, or smells, but it could also be more specific things, such as a nanny's necklace or a parent's sweater. This can also include acts like breastfeeding (see adult breastfeeding, page 9), wearing diapers (see adult baby, page 8), or being spanked.

anal beads

A sex toy consisting of a string of beads, typically made of either silicone, plastic, or glass, with space in between each bead. The string is inserted into the anus, then gently removed by pulling on the exposed end, allowing one bead at a time to pass through the anus.

anal bumper cars

A very challenging anal sex position. Both partners lie on their stomachs, facing opposite directions, with the giving partner on top; both partners' heads should be near the other partner's feet. The receiving partner opens their legs a bit. The giving partner positions their genitals or a toy on top of the receiver's backside and inserts it into the anus.

anal hook
A sex toy; a curved metal object with a sphere or multiple spheres on the hook end and a ring on the other end for easy holding. The hook end is inserted into the anus and is used to stimulate the prostate or sphincter.

anal play
The term for any sexual stimulation involving the anus.

anal sex
Sexual intercourse involving the anus, specifically when the anus is penetrated either by a penis or toy. Anal sex can be extremely pleasurable, as there are nerve endings that run up and down the anal cavity, and penetration can stimulate the prostate (see page 139) or even the G-spot (see page 69).

In the past few decades, anal sex has gone from a taboo subject to a more widely experienced type of intercourse. Of course, there are still stigmas surrounding the act, as well as fear of uncleanliness or pain, but these things can be taken care of easily if anal sex is something you would like to experience.

Take the advice of porn star Asa Akira, who is widely referred to as the "queen of anal sex." Here are some tips she has for those who would like to try anal sex:

For the receiving partner:

Start by making sure that your anal cavity is clean. For this purpose, Asa likes to employ an enema, which is a bag filled with water with a thin hose attached. Use the hose to very slowly fill your anus with water, a little bit at a time; you should feel when you can't fit any more water. Then, remove the hose and let the water drain out. Repeat the process until the water runs clear.

Use butt plugs of varying sizes to train your anus to open and accept penetrating objects. Start with a small one and insert it for a short period of time. Then remove it and use a larger one. If you feel pain, stop. This process can take a few weeks.

Drink psyllium husk to help clean your system.

Lubrication is key! There are many types of lubricants out there; silicone lube is the most recommended kind for skin-to-skin insertion, but if you are using a toy, check its packaging to see what kind of lube (silicone or water-based) you should be using.

For the giving partner:

When your partner is ready for the first experience, remember to *slowly* insert the object you are using. Let the receiving partner initiate all of the movement, even though it might be tempting for you to move. This will make the experience much more comfortable for both parties.

Don't forget encouragement! Kind words and obvious enjoyment will help your partner feel confident.

analingus
A type of oral sex in which the tongue and mouth are used to stimulate the anus.

anasteemaphilia
Someone with a sexual preference for a partner who is significantly taller or shorter than they are. (Also see macrophilia, page 95, and microphilia, page 98).

androidism
A fetish for robots that are specifically designed to look like humans, a.k.a. androids. Pseudo-androidism is the sexual practice of pretending one is a robot.

androsexual
Those who have a sexual preference for partners who identify as male. This term is often used by those who are genderqueer in order to express their preference without assigning themselves a gender.

angry dragon
An oral sex act in which the giving partner ejaculates into the receiving partner's mouth, then moves the receiver's head forward so that the ejaculate travels through the throat and out the nose, giving the appearance of an angry, smoke-breathing dragon.

animal play

A type of role-play in which one or both partners pretend to be animals. Animal play is often practiced in BDSM relationships, where the Master (see page 97) has the slave (see page 182) act as a dog or other leashed animal. This is not related to bestiality (see page 233), as it is always understood that this is fantasy and partners involved are always human.

anonymous sex

A consensual sexual encounter of any kind that happens between people who have never met before and do not wish to know each other after completion.

anophelorastia

A fantasy fetish that causes one to experience arousal from thinking about defiling their partner's body. This fetish is entirely in the imagination and does not extend to physical harm.

antholagnia

A sexual preference where a person experiences arousal from the sight, aroma, thought, or touch of flowers.

Flowers are often seen as signs of love—they have beautiful and unique shapes, colors, and smells, just like we do! It's no wonder that flowers are a preferred gift from a partner looking to spark some romance. But did you know that there is actual scientific backing that says women may be more likely to agree to a date when asked in the presence of flowers? In a 2011 study from France published in the scientific journal *Social Influence*, a group of female participants entered a room, one at a time, where they were shown video profiles of both typically attractive and unattractive men. For half of the women, the room was decorated with a few vases of flowers; for the other half, the room was decorated normally. When asked to rate their attraction to each man and their willingness to date each one, the women who were in the room with the flowers rated the men as significantly more attractive than did the women in the room without flowers, and expressed more willingness to date them. So can flowers truly help love bloom? Maybe, but science says it's definitely worth a shot!

---

apocalypse sex

Frenzied sexual activities that take place when there is an incoming catastrophic disaster. Disasters like tsunamis or fires can come on suddenly and give little time to escape to safety. Some people feel like there's no point in trying to escape, so they use the time to have sex, possibly trying something they've always wanted to try in the face of imminent destruction. Also called end-of-the-world sex.

aquaphilia

Literally translated as "love of water," aquaphilia is a fetish that causes one to experience intense sexual arousal when exposed to water or when watching one's partner interact with water.

arachnophilia
A type of zoophilia (see page 231) in which a person has an extreme attraction to spiders.

arch position
A penetrative sex position where the receiving partner starts by lying on their back, then lifts their lower body into the air, keeping shoulders and arms on the ground. The giving partner grabs the receiver's legs and positions their genitals together, creating an arch.

armbinder
A device used in BDSM (see page ix) or sadomasochism (see page 160) that restrains a submissive's or slave's arms behind their back. The device is different from typical bindings like rope or handcuffs in that it binds the majority of the arms, not just the wrists.

Around the World
1. A term for intercourse that utilizes several different sexual positions before completion.

2. The sexual act of kissing, licking, or otherwise orally stimulating a partner's entire body prior to giving oral sex.

asexuality
A lack of any type of sexual attraction, arousal, or interest in pursuing any sexual experience. Asexual people can still experience romantic love, and often enter into relationships to fulfill that need. Some people are both aromantic and asexual, and have no desire for sex or romantic love.

Asiaphile
A person who is not of Asian descent who has a fetish or preference for partners of Asian descent.

asphyxiophilia
A fetish for a reduced exposure to oxygen, which is said to heighten sexual experience and orgasm. People with this fetish practice intense breath control during intercourse. This fetish is often associated with autoerotic asphyxiation, a masturbatory technique of cutting off access to oxygen (typically through self-strangulation) when in the throes of orgasm.

* Note: limiting your exposure to oxygen can cause fainting, or in extreme cases death. If you decide to practice asphyxiophilia, we highly suggest either letting someone know what you're planning on ahead of time, or having a spotter in the room with you.

ass job
A sex act in which the penis is placed between the other partner's butt cheeks, which are then used to masturbate.

ass-to-mouth
The term for any sexual activity where a mouth makes contact with someone else's backside, specifically on the anal opening. (Also see rim job page 154).

asstronaut
A slang term for a giving partner experienced with anal sex (see page 19) who has anal sex with a receiving partner who has not yet experienced it.

asthenolagnia
A fetish for feeling weak or humiliated.

Australian kiss
A slang term for cunnilingus, as it refers to going "down under."

autassassinophilia
A fetish for the idea or imminent threat of being killed, especially during intercourse. Some autassassinophiliacs experience arousal simply by thinking about their death, but it must specifically be *their* death, and not the general idea of death.

autocunnilingus
A very challenging masturbatory act in which a person with a vagina uses their own mouth to stimulate their genitals.

autoeroticism

1. The state of being intensely attracted to oneself. Auto-erotic people prefer masturbation to partnered sex.

2. The act of reaching sexual completion without outside stimuli, using only one's own body and imagination.

autofellatio

A very challenging masturbatory act in which a person with a penis uses their own mouth to stimulate their genitals.

autopederasty

An extremely challenging stimulation technique in which a person with a long penis inserts it into their own anus. It is unclear whether ejaculation can occur from this technique.

autosadism

A fetish for causing oneself physical pain.

B

B&D
1. The BDSM acronym for "bondage & discipline," a sex act that employs physical restraints along with orders or rules that the bound person must follow. Bondage & discipline does not necessarily involve physical pain.

2. The BDSM acronym for "bondage & domination," a sex act where a person is bound and then dominated, usually in a pain/pleasure scenario.

backdoor man
A slang term for a gay man who prefers to be the giving partner. (Also see top, page 207).

ball-busting
Any sexual act in which physical harm is done to a partner's testicles, such as through binding, squeezing, punching,

or kicking. People on the extreme side have been known to have their testes hurt with whips, hammers, paddles, and other BDSM devices. (Also see algolagnia, page 14, and tamakeri, page 200).

ball gag
A BDSM sex toy. Ball gags are round or oval balls, typically made of rubber or plastic, that have a strap on each side. The ball is inserted into a submissive's mouth and the straps tied around their head to prevent movement of the ball.

ball hood
A BDSM sensory deprivation device meant to restrict all of a submissive's senses. The collar is fastened around a submissive's neck and the hood is inflated like a beach ball. The inflatable portion is made of two layers of plastic or rubber, with air flowing between the two layers, putting more pressure on the wearer's head. The wearer breathes through a tube that extends out from the hood.

ball tie bondage position
A BDSM penetrative sex position in which the receiving partner curls up into a ball (almost in a fetal position), and their wrists are then bound to their ankles, allowing the giving partner easy access to any available insertion points.

balloon fetish
A fetish that causes one to experience arousal when inflating, popping, or coming into contact with balloons. This is a type of inflatophilia (see page 84).

Think having a sexual attraction to balloons is loony? Those with a balloon fetish might agree with you! People with this fetish affectionately call themselves "looners." The looner community is surprisingly large and very active. Looners often host "popping parties" (where attendees pop balloons with their hands, backs, or other instruments) and classes on how to purposefully move your body in a sexual way while on a balloon. There are many online forums and blogs dedicated to balloon love.

---

bang
A slang term for having sexual intercourse.

bareback sex
Sex without condoms. Having bareback sex increases your risk for pregnancy and STIs.

bastinado
A BDSM sex act where the bottoms of a submissive's feet are exposed and then whipped, paddled, or thrashed. This is a type of pain play (see page 112).

BBW
An acronym for "big beautiful woman." This refers to a woman who has an above average weight, and is used by those who fetishize or have a sexual preference for such women. This could mean women who are slightly overweight or those who are obese; there isn't a set definition for this fetish, and it is up to the fetishist to determine where the BBW line starts for them.

bedroom eyes
A seductive look given to a partner in order to arouse them or suggest intercourse. Also known as "come-hither eyes."

belonephilia
A fetish for sharp objects, such as pins, knives, swords, or scissors.

bench player position
A penetrative sex position with a medium level of difficulty. The giving partner sits on a bench or chair and spreads their legs slightly. The receiving partner then lowers themself onto the giving partner, facing the same way as the giving partner, resulting in direct penetration.

Berkley Horse
A type of BDSM furniture designed to assist in the flogging of submissives. The piece is shaped like a rack, with a hole up top for the head to poke through, and holes down

near the bottom to access the person's genitals, giving way to the perfect balance of pain and pleasure.

The Berkley Horse was designed in 1828 by an English dominatrix named Theresa Berkley. She was widely known as a master of torture (she was about as famous as a mainstream porn star would be today) and attracted many customers in the English aristocracy, though she was extremely private about her client list. However, upon her death it was discovered that she did keep letters from some of her more prominent customers, and some say that there were even letters from members of the royal family in her collection. But since her estate was escheated to the crown after her brother and her medical attendant both refused administration duties, the letters were apparently destroyed, so we'll never know which high-born English folks were really into getting tied up and flogged.

BFP
This BDSM term is an acronym for "bound for pleasure" and refers to submissives who find pleasure in being bound or tied.

birth control
Any method used to prevent pregnancy during sex, including condoms, IUDs, birth control pills, the pull-out method (see page 143), and other contraceptives.

bisexual
A term for those who feel sexual and romantic attraction to two types of genders; this generally (though not always) means men and women.

black sheet party
A slang term for an orgy hosted specifically for BDSM participants.

blood play
The term for involving blood in some way during sexual activity. This could be bloodletting, drinking blood, or simply being in the presence of blood. (Also see hematolagnia page 77).

blow job
Often abbreviated as "BJ," this is a slang term for fellatio, or oral sex performed on a penis.

blumpkin
A sex act in which fellatio is performed on a recipient while the recipient is defecating in a toilet.

body fluid monogamy
A sexual lifestyle in which a committed couple practices unprotected sex with each other. In some cases the partners may also experience protected sex outside of the relationship, without the exchange of any bodily fluid. Couples

in this lifestyle can be referred to as fluid-bonded. Many believe that this type of relationship enhances intimacy between partners, though there is no scientific backing for this statement.

bondage cuffs
A BDSM sex toy designed to restrain a person's wrists or ankles. Unlike traditional handcuffs, bondage cuffs are typically made of leather and are often padded for the comfort of the person being restrained.

boob job
A sex act in which a penis, toy, or other object is inserted between the breasts, and then the breasts are used to masturbate that object.

booster seat position
A very challenging sex position in which the receiving partner squats as if they are going to sit back in a chair. The giving partner holds the receiving partner in this position with their arms and inserts themself into the receiving partner. This is best used for anal intercourse.

bottom
A slang term for a person who prefers to be a receiving partner during intercourse.

boundaries
A term that describes the limits of a person's sexual preferences. Especially important in BDSM relationships, boundaries are always discussed before entering a new Master/slave relationship, or before performing any sex act where pain or discomfort of any kind may be involved.

bra fetish
A fetish that causes one to experience extreme sexual arousal when seeing a bra, wearing a bra, or seeing a partner's breasts in a bra. Most bra fetishists prefer seeing breasts in bras to seeing naked breasts. This is a type of clothing fetish (see page 41).

brank
A BDSM sex toy; a frame-like device that is placed on a submissive's head and used to restrain the tongue. Branks were often used as torture devices in medieval times.

breast bondage
A type of sex play in which a partner's breasts are tied with rope, sometimes cutting off blood flow to the breast tissue. This act is more focused on the visual aspect of tied breasts than on restraint.

breeding fetish
A fetish for impregnating a partner or for being impregnated. Those with breeding fetishes will often refer to

themself or their partner by parental terms such as Daddy or Mommy. Breeding fetishes are a type of maiesiophilia (see page 96).

bridal fetish
A fetish for brides or women dressed up in bridal apparel. There is speculation that this fetish stems from the fact that brides are a traditional symbol of virginity (see virgin fetish, page 219), but it is more typically seen as an attraction to bridal adornments and acts.

bridge position
A penetrative sex position in which the receiving partner makes a bridge with their body, holding up their torso, hips, and groin with their arms and legs. The giving partner kneels between the receiving partner's knees and supports the receiving partner with their hands. This is similar to the arch position (see page 22) in reverse.

brothel
Also known as a bordello or whorehouse, this is the term for a business where one can go to purchase and experience time with a prostitute.

bukkake
A sex act in which a group of people with penises stand around someone who is sitting and masturbate until they orgasm onto the sitting person's body.

burping fetish
A fetish for the sound—or, less commonly, the act—of burping.

butt plug
A sex toy which is used to stimulate the anus. Made in a conical shape with a wide, flat portion at the end to prevent a swallowing effect, these toys are meant to be left in the anus for extended periods of time. They are often decorated on the flat end with jewels, images, or even tails. Butt plugs are also used to train an anus to open for anal intercourse.

C

candaulism

A fetish for showing off your partner either naked or during sexual intercourse (whether live or through pictures or video). This is related to voyeurism (see page 220).

Candaulism was named after the Greek king Candaules and the story of his fetish told in Herodotus' *Histories*. As the story goes, Candaules was having trouble convincing his bodyguard, Gyges, that his wife, Queen Nyssia, was more beautiful than any woman in the world, and so he devised a plan to have Gyges see Nyssia naked. Against Gyges' protests, Candaules made him hide behind a door in the royal bedchamber, and when Nyssia took off her robe to get into bed, Gyges saw her naked body. However, Nyssia spotted Gyges in his hiding place, and, utterly embarrassed, swore revenge on her husband. The next day, Nyssia confronted Gyges and demanded that he choose to kill either himself or Candaules as punishment for their crime. Though Gyges begged not to be made to choose, Nyssia wore him down until he consented to murder Candaules in the same way in which she was shamed; Gyges hid behind a door in the bedchamber and killed the king in his sleep. Gyges and Nyssia then married, which began the Mermnad Dynasty. While there is a lot of argument over the validity of this story, the moral lesson is clear: Always have consent from your partner before showing them off in any sexual way.

---

cartwheel position

A very challenging penetrative sex position in which the receiving partner stands on their hands, as if in the middle of a cartwheel. The giving partner grabs the receiving partner's legs for support and inserts themselves into the giving partner.

castration fantasy

A fetish for castration, whether for the removal of one's own testicles or for the act of removing a partner's testicles. The fetish specifically centers on the act of castration, and does not include a preference for those who are already castrated.

casual sex

The term for any sex act that takes place outside of an established relationship, such as one-night stands (see page 106) or anonymous sex (see page 20).

CAT

An acronym that stands for "coital alignment technique," a sex act in which the partners are in missionary position (see page 98), but instead of penetrating the receiving partner, the giving partner uses their penis or an object to stimulate the receiver's genitals. This works particularly well for receiving partners with a clitoris, as it will cause direct stimulation.

catamite

The term for a younger man who is the receiving partner in gay relationships.

catcher

A slang term for the receiving partner in anal sex.

catheterophilia

A fetish for having a catheter, a flexible plastic tube which aids in the removal of bodily fluids, inserted into one's body. This is *not* a fetish for partners with a catheter.

CBT

An acronym for "cock and ball torture," which is a BDSM term for inflicting pain on the penis and testicles. Typically, this involves the penis and testicles being restrained in some way, but it can also involve hitting, whipping, or paddling them.

chair bondage
The BDSM term for binding a submissive to a chair for any type of sexual activity.

chastity
A term used to describe acting within the sexual boundaries of one's religion or culture, such as not having sex before marriage, or only having sex on certain days of the week. In modern times, this word is often used as a synonym for abstinence (see page 6).

chastity belt
A sexual device used to obstruct one's genitals. It consists of metal underwear that can be locked, with an opening near the genitals that can let out bodily fluids, but not let in a penis or other object. In medieval times these were used to protect women from being raped, or, more commonly, to prevent premarital sex. In modern times, chastity belts are used by the BDSM community as a tool of dominance.

chemical play
The term for any sex act in which partners use some sort of chemical (a refined substance) during intercourse. Different chemicals cause different reactions; some, such as the herbal tincture Tiger Balm, are pleasurable, and some, such as chili oil, cause pain. This can also relate to food play (see page 65) when food items such as hot sauces are used.

choreophilia
A fetish for dancing or for watching others dance.

chrematistophilia
1. A fetish for the act or thought of paying for sex.
2. A fetish for being robbed or for losing one's possessions. Often referred to as the "hold-up kink."

chrysophilia
A fetish for gold or gold-tinted objects. Chrysophiliacs will often wear gold jewelry or other gold clothing items during intercourse.

circle jerk
A sex act in which a group of people stand in a circle and masturbate themselves or one another until ejaculation.

claustrophilia
A fetish for being confined to small spaces. This does not necessarily include seeing one's partner in a small space.

cleaning fetish
A fetish for the act of cleaning or seeing one's partner clean something.

clitoris
A sensitive part of the vulva (page 220), which sits just above the urethra.

Of all the sexual body parts, none seem to transmit more feelings of confusion than the clitoris. But the clitoris is actually pretty easy to understand; it's an organ solely designed for pleasure that sits at the top of the vulva. Like the penis, it's extremely sensitive—it has over 8,000 nerve endings, actually double the amount that a penis has! It's shaped like a wishbone, the top glans sticking out of the body (the telltale nub) while the rest of the clitoris is inside the body, running down either end of the labia minora. Many people with clitorises love to have them stimulated during sexual encounters, and some even have orgasms solely from clitoral stimulation alone!

clothing fetish
A fetish for clothing (one's own or a partner's), or for a specific article or style of clothing. One well-known type of clothing fetish is a bra fetish (see page 33).

cock gagging
A form of oral sex in which the receiving partner inserts their genitals deep into the giving partner's mouth, causing them to gag or (in extreme cases) to vomit.

cock ring
A sex toy; a rubber, metal, or plastic ring which is slipped onto an erect penis and typically placed at the base. The cock ring will restrict blood flow, allowing the user to maintain an erection for an extended period of time.

Vibrating cock rings, which can stimulate the user's shaft and scrotum, are also available.

chronophilia
A fetish for people who fall into a specific age range. For example, a chronophiliac might be attracted to people who are between the ages of twenty-seven and twenty-nine, but no older or younger.

coitus
The scientific term for any sex act that involves penetrative intercourse between a partner with a penis and a partner with a vagina and ends in ejaculation. This term is typically applied when talking about traditional views of conception or pregnancy.

collar fetish
A fetish for wearing a collar and experiencing the feeling of being "owned" by someone, or for seeing one's partner in a collar and "owning" them. A "collar" can be anything that symbolizes the wearer's submission to their owner, but it is always a worn object.

condom
A contraceptive and sexual protection tool used during intercourse. Made of latex, polyurethane, or animal intestine, this thin, sheath-like object is rolled over a penis or other object before vaginal, anal, or oral penetration.

coprophilia
The fetish for eating feces, or for watching a partner eat feces.

copulation
A scientific term for any form of penetrative intercourse. Similar to coitus (see page 42), but for any gender(s).

corduroy fetish
Someone with a fetish for the material corduroy. (Also see clothing fetish, page 41).

coregasm
An orgasm that is induced by exercise. Coregasms are often experienced by those with kinesophilia (see page 89), but may also simply occur during a very pleasurable type of exercise.

corporal punishment
A BDSM term for any kind of physical harm that is inflicted upon a submissive or slave. Often abbreviated as "CP."

corset fetish
A fetish for wearing a corset or for seeing a partner wear a corset. This is a fairly common fetish in the BDSM community.

cottaging
A slang term for anonymous sex between two men in a public area.

coulrophilia
An extreme attraction to clowns and the act of clowning. Coulrophilia can also apply to street performers or other vaudevillian performers who wear heavy makeup and exaggerated clothing.

cowgirl position
An easy penetrative sex position in which the giving partner lies on their back and the receiving partner straddles the giver and initiates penetration. This gives the receiving partner a lot of control over the speed and depth of penetration.

cradle position
An easy anal sex position in which the receiving partner lies on their back, lifts their legs in the air, and rests their legs on the giver's shoulders. The giver can then lift and support the receiver's bottom and initiate penetration.

cream pie
A sex act in which one partner ejaculates into the other and then allows the sexual fluid to fall out. A common misconception is that those with a cream pie fetish also have a breeding fetish (see page 33), since both involve unprotected penile ejaculation, but with cream pies, the ejaculate falls out of the receiver, whereas in breeding, it stays inside.

cross-eyed fetish

A fetish for people who have crossed eyes.

René Descartes, the famous French philosopher, had an intense love of cross-eyed women, which began in childhood and stretched into his formative years. However, it is speculated that René was embarrassed by his love for crossed eyes, and so he decided to track his fetish back to where it first began: a cute, childhood playmate. By meditating on the start of the fetish, he claims to have rid himself of it. This act of changing his attraction actually inspired the third part of his moral maxim: you need to master oneself, rather than the outside world, in order to create change in one's desires.

---

cross-orientation play

A scenario where people have sex with partners they are not normally sexually oriented towards. These scenarios don't occur often, but they might come about as the result of an order in a BDSM or Master/slave relationship.

crurophilia

A fetish for legs, either one's own or a partner's.

crushing fetish

A fetish for the act of crushing or being crushed. This can involve crushing small insects, but typically focuses on inanimate objects or people. Someone with this fetish might enjoy being stepped on or having heavy objects placed on top of them.

cuckcake
The female version of a cuckold; a woman who likes to watch her partner have sex with other women.

cuckold
A person in a committed relationship who watches their partner have sex with someone outside of the relationship. This typically refers to a man who likes to have his female partner have sex with other men, but it can be applied to any gender.

cum swapping
Typically seen in pornography or practiced during threesomes, cum swapping is a sex act in which one person puts the ejaculate of a partner into their mouth, then transfers it to another partner while kissing them. Also see snowballing (page 186).

cumming
The slang term for having an orgasm or ejaculating.

cunnilingus
The technical term for oral sex performed on somebody with a vagina.

cunt
A slang word for *vagina,* often considered derogatory.

> The word that most dare not say; the dreaded C-word. This word, which originally simply meant *vagina,* morphed into something so offensive that to utter it causes panic within our society; the reason for this is still unknown. But what is fascinating is that many of today's feminists are now embracing the word as a symbol of sexual freedom, much as the LGBT community has done with the word "queer." While many still consider "cunt" a taboo word, these women use it to describe themselves and their vaginas. They put forth all of their pride and love for their gender in this one culturally "obscene" word. You can now find the word "cunt" in pop culture, songs, books, and movies, which is pretty incredible considering that even twenty years ago, careers could be ended by even thinking of the word.

cut
The slang term for a circumcised penis.

cyber sex
The term for any sex act which utilizes a computer or the Internet, such as naughty chat room conversations or web camera exchanges.

cyprieunia
The term for having paid sex with a sex worker.

D

dacryphilia
A fetish for the act of crying or for seeing others cry. Dacryphilia is a common fetish of sadists, who enjoy seeing the physical manifestation of their partner's pain. Also related to hygrophilia (see page 80).

Daddy
A BDSM term for an older partner, typically male, who takes on an authoritative and protective role. This is most often seen in daddy/little girl relationships, where both partners are people of legal age who are role-playing a part.

daisy chain
A sex act in which at least three people perform oral sex on each other at the same time.

dancewear fetish
A fetish for clothing worn during professional dancing, such as leotards, tutus, or ballet shoes.

Danza slap
A slang term for an oral sex act in which a receiving partner with a penis removes it from the receiver's mouth and slaps it on the giving partner's face.

DDF
Acronym for "drug and disease free." This is a common phrase used on dating and sex-finding apps, websites, and personal listings.

deep-throating
An oral sex act in which a penis or other sex object is inserted so far into the giving partner's mouth, it penetrates their throat.

deflowering
A slang term for having sex with a virgin for the first time.

demiromantic
A person who can only form romantic connections with someone once an emotional connection has been made. They do not experience "love at first sight" or on-sight attraction.

dendrophilia
A fetish for trees, especially the thought or act of having intercourse with a tree.

desensitizer
A cream or gel that is applied to an area of the body to numb it. For sex acts, desensitizers are typically used either to numb a penis to delay ejaculation or to numb an orifice to make penetration more comfortable.

detumescence
The scientific term for the stage when blood leaves the penis after an erection and the penis becomes flaccid.

devil's threesome
A threesome with two men and one woman.

diddle
The slang term for digital stimulation of the vagina.

dildo
Any phallic object designed for penetration.

Just as there are hundreds of different penis types in the world, dildos come in all different shapes, colors, and sizes. There are dildos meant specifically for anal sex, with bulbous heads meant to stay in an anal cavity; there are double dildos, which have an insertion point on each end and can be great for two partners with vaginas; there are dildos meant to reach a G-spot, dildos made of glass for different tactile sensations, vibrating dildos, and dildos that can simulate ejaculation. There are even dildos for dracophiliacs (see page 53) that are shaped like imagined dragon penises. The world of dildos is vast and incredible, and if you like penetration, there is definitely a dildo out there for you.

---

doggy style position

A penetrative sex position in which the receiving partner gets down on their hands and knees and the giving partner penetrates them from behind, simulating the way dogs and other four-legged mammals typically have sex.

dollification

A fetish for dressing up as a doll or for having a partner dress up like a doll. This process typically involves makeup and costumes, but on the extreme side it can involve plastic surgery to make one's body "perfect," like a doll's.

dominatrix

1. A name for a female dominant in a BDSM relationship.

2. The term for a female sex worker who specializes in administration of pain.

Don Juanism
A fetish for having sex with as many different partners as possible. For Don Juans, arousal comes more from the conquest (getting someone into bed) than from the sex itself.

dong
A slang term for a penis or dildo.

doppelbanger
A play on the word "doppelganger," this is a term used to describe a person you would like to have sex with solely because they look like someone else.

doraphilia
A fetish for touching fur, leather, or skin. The skin does not necessarily have to be attached to a living creature, as in the case of leather, but it does need to be real skin.

double bedder
1. The act of having two instances of casual sex in one day.

2. A person who is so attractive that people who normally prefer one-night stands would sleep with them twice.

double blow job
A blow job (see page 31) that is performed by two givers at once on one receiver.

double penetration
The term for a sex act in which a receiving partner is penetrated both vaginally and anally at the same time. In pornography, this is referred to by the acronym "DP."

dracophilia
A fetish for dragons. Since dragons don't actually exist, people with this fetish do a lot of role-playing, interaction with dragon toys, or looking at erotic art involving dragons.

dry humping
A type of outercourse in which partners will rub their genitals against one another while wearing clothing.

DSL
An acronym for the slang term "dick-sucking lips," which describes a set of very full lips that would be good for fellatio.

DTF
Slang acronym for "down to fuck," meaning that someone is open to having intercourse.

dysmorphophilia
A fetish or sexual preference for people with mental or physical impairments.

dyspareunia
A term for any sexual act which is painful or causes physical discomfort.

E

eating out
A slang term for cunnilingus (see page 46), or performing oral sex on a vagina.

ecosexual
A fetish for nature and naturally occurring objects or areas, such as oceans or forests.

ederacinism
A fetish for the thought of removing one's own sexual organs.

edgeplay
A BDSM term for any sex act that borders the edge of safety or sanity either physically or mentally. Since everyone has different boundaries, this term is extremely subjective, as it is up to an individual to decide what is safe for them.

edging
Also known as orgasm control, edging is a sex act in which someone is brought to the brink of orgasm during a sexual experience, and then their partner will slow or stop the sexual activity in order to prolong and intensify the release.

ejaculate
The seminal fluid that is released from the testes and penis upon orgasm.

ejaculation
The act of expelling ejaculate from the penis during orgasm.

electrophilia
A fetish for electricity; specifically, getting electric shocks on one's body or administering electric shocks on a partner's body. Electrophiliacs will often participate in erotic electrostimulation (see page 58).

emetophilia
The term for a vomit fetish, particularly watching one's partner vomit. This is very common with gagging fetishes.

endytophilia
A fetish for having sex while one or both partners are wearing clothing. This could also be related to a clothing fetish (see page 41).

entomophilia
A fetish for insects. This can include holding insects, seeing insects, or sometimes even eating insects.

ephebophilia
A fetish or sexual preference for adolescents. Typically, an ephebophiliac will be attracted to those between ages fifteen and nineteen, but it does vary. This is a type of chronophilia (see page 42).

eproctolagniac
Someone who is aroused by the sound or smell of flatulence. This fetish is also known as flatulophilia.

erection
The term for the physical lengthening and engorging of a penis caused by a rush of blood to the organ, which makes it firm.

The process by which a penis goes from flaccid to erect is absolutely fascinating. It's not just blood flowing into veins of the penis—as you know, blood flows through veins all over our body, but flows right back out again at the same speed. So, how do penises reach and retain their trademark firmness? It all starts in the brain, where a burst of a neurotransmitter called nitric oxide causes a muscle enzyme to produce a body messenger called cyclic guanine monophosphate (cGMP). At the same time, the body's arteries expand and the veins contract. cGMP races

down those arteries and increases the size of the blood vessels that are carrying blood to the penis along the way. When the blood reaches the penis, it fills the spaces of the corpora cavernosa, two sponge-like tissue chambers that run from the head of the penis to the inside of the pelvis. The corpora cavernosa utilize pressure to keep the blood inside the penis, and with the veins contracted, it means that the blood is also entering much faster than it leaves, allowing the penis to stay firm for long periods of time!

---

erogenous zone

An area of the body that has a higher concentration of nerve endings and is often associated with sexual stimulation. Erogenous zones include genitals, lips, nipples, and even ears.

erotic electrostimulation

The use of electricity during sexual play. Electricity is generally administered to the body through the use of specially designed sex toys, such as neon wands, which discharge static electricity when applied to skin, or a TENS (transcutaneous electrical nerve stimulation) unit, which administers controlled bits of electricity using pads attached to the body.

erotic enema

A sex act practiced in BDSM circles in which a submissive or slave is given an enema during sexual activity.

erotica
A literary or artistic work that focuses on a sexual act or feeling.

erotocomatose lucidity
Typically abbreviated as "ECL," this is a state of blissful exhaustion that is entered after partners have had a lot of sex, prolonging orgasm, with small breaks in between each session. This is said to open the mind, and is used in some occult circles to better communicate with spirits.

erotographomania
A fetish for the act of writing, particularly erotica or romantic literature.

erotophilia
A general term for a positive relationship with sex. Erotophiliacs usually have more sex in their lives and have an openness to many different sexual acts.

erotophobia
The opposite of erotophilia; a general term for a fear of sex. This encompasses people who have specific sex phobias as well as those who are fearful of anything related to sex.

exhibitionism
A fetish for exposing one's body to others in a sexual manner. Exhibitionism takes many forms, from streaking

to having sex in public places (see agoraphilia, page 13). Many porn stars are exhibitionists. (Also see agrexophilia, page 13).

eye-fucking
A slang term for looking at someone in a way that expresses sexual desire. Also known as "undressing someone with your eyes."

F

facesitting

A sex act in which one partner sits on another partner's face in order to receive oral sex or analingus (see page 19). This is a common practice in BDSM, where the dominant partner will sit on the submissive's face as a form of erotic humiliation.

facial

A slang term for ejaculating (see page 56) on a partner's face.

If you've ever explored the wide world of pornography, you'll notice that a stunning amount of videos end with facials in lieu of any other kind of completion. But why is that? Two reasons seem to be the most logical: 1) because pornography is such an exaggerated form of sex and it lasts much longer than a typical sex session, many porn stars with penises train themselves to last for extended periods of time and also to ejaculate on demand. Ejaculating on command is much easier using the "jerk to pop" method, where the penis is manually stimulated; 2) there is an emphasis on the degradation of the facial act for both parties, which definitely features heavily in produced pornography. However, it could be simple supply and demand; maybe millions of people who watch porn love facials, which causes the porn creators to write in more of them.

fear play
The general term for any sex act that utilizes fear to elicit a sexual response.

felching
A slang term for the act of licking or sucking semen out of an orifice.

fellatio
The technical term for oral sex that is performed on a penis. Often referred to as a blow job.

fembot
A robot that is designed to anatomically resemble a human female, often used as a sexual object. Because of the cost required to make them extremely lifelike, they are very rare.

femdom
A shortened form of "female dominance." This is a BDSM term for a relationship where the dominant partner, or dominatrix (see page 51), is female.

female ejaculation
Also known as squirting, this is the term for when a vagina releases a colorless, odorless fluid when experiencing sexual stimulation or orgasm.

female muscle fetish
A fetish for muscular women.

feminist pornography
A genre of pornography produced specifically for female viewers. The focus of feminist pornography tends to be the freedom of female sexuality.

fetish wear
Clothing that is designed to be worn for sexual purposes. Fetish wear is often made of materials such as rubber, leather, or latex and is cut to cling and accentuate one's body shape.

figging
A BDSM sex act in which a piece of shaved ginger root is inserted into a submissive's anus. The ginger causes a burning sensation in the sensitive areas of the anus, but does not cause any actual harm.

fingering
The act of using one's fingers to stimulate a partner's genitals, particularly a vagina (including the labia and clitoris) or anus.

fire play
The term for any sex act that uses fire to elicit a sexual response, such as placing lit candles near a person's skin, or rubbing alcohol on skin, then igniting it and extinguishing it very quickly. Note: If you or your partner are interested in experimenting with fire play, remember to always have a fire extinguisher or fire blanket close by.

fisting
A sex act in which an entire hand is inserted into the anus or vagina. Contrary to popular belief, the inserted hand is not actually in a fist position during insertion or stimulation; rather, all five fingers are held together with the fingertips as close together as possible. This allows the hand to glide in more easily.

flagellation
The act of whipping or striking a person for the sexual satisfaction of either the person doing the whipping or the person being whipped (or both). This is a very common practice in BDSM relationships.

flicking the bean
A slang term for female masturbation. The "bean" is slang for the clitoris.

flogger
A BDSM sex toy; a type of whip that has multiple tails. This type of toy is not meant to inflict severe pain, but rather to heighten sensitivity for the person being whipped.

food play
The term for any sex act where food is used in a sexual manner, including feeding a partner in a sexy way, using aphrodisiacs, or rubbing food on a partner's body. (Also see sitophilia, page 180).

foot fetish
An intense attraction to feet. A person with a foot fetish might like particular sizes or shapes of feet, or might have a preference for feet adorned with jewelry, such as toe rings or anklets.

The fetish for feet is more common than you'd think, and in fact, there are plenty of celebrities and public figures who readily admit their love for our most grounded body parts. The author F. Scott Fitzgerald was a well-known foot fetishist; he often visited a particular prostitute whose feet, he said, were so incredibly beautiful he could hardly bear to part from them. Elvis Presley was also said to have

a fondness for feet, and any lady hoping to have a private meeting with him first had to have her feet checked for optimal attractiveness. In the modern world, pop musician Pharrell Williams very openly talks about his love for women's feet. He and his N*E*R*D bandmate Shae share the same fetish, and one can only imagine the conversation they'd have about an attractive fan's feet.

---

foot job
A sex act in which feet are used to masturbate a partner's genitals.

formicophilia
A type of entomophilia (see page 57) in which someone gets sexual satisfaction from insects crawling on or inside their genitals.

fourgy
A slang term for an orgy that includes four participants.

fourth base
A slang term for penetrative intercourse, which many consider to be the point where a physical relationship becomes truly sexual.

freckle fetish
A fetish for people with freckled skin.

friends with benefits
A slang term for two or more people who have regular sexual encounters with each other but do not engage in romantic feelings or activities.

frog squat
A penetrative sex position that's similar to cowgirl position. The difference for this position is that the receiver's feet are planted on the ground instead of their knees.

frottage
Also known as sexual rubbing, frottage is a sex act in which two partners rub their genitals against one another's in order to reach climax. When both partners have penises, the act is referred to as frication, and when both partners have vaginas/vulvas, it is called tribadism.

fuck buddy
The slang term for someone with whom one has a sexual relationship while still maintaining a friendship, without the development of romantic emotion.

fuck stick
A slang term for a penis.

furry
A person with a strong fascination and admiration for anthropomorphic animals (animals that have human

qualities, such as wearing clothes and holding jobs). This can include visualizing oneself as an anthropomorphic animal or wearing a costume known as a fursuit. While furries do not always extend their obsession to sexual activities, some do. Sexual activity between furries is called yiffing (see page 229).

G

G-spot
An erogenous zone located inside the vagina, possibly one to two inches deep. This can be an extremely sensitive spot for some women.

gag
A BDSM sex toy; any device that is inserted into the mouth to prevent a submissive from speaking.

gangbang
The term for a group sex experience, where one person has sex with everyone else at the group, who often stimulates or has sex with multiple people in that group at a time.

gay
The term that describes a man who is strictly attracted to other men.

gerontophilia

A fetish or sexual preference for people who are older than oneself.

MILFs, DILFs, and silver foxes—just why is the attraction to older people so popular? While most media tends to paint a picture of an Oedipus-like situation, where younger, sexually active people look for those who remind them of their parents, the truth seems to rest more on one uniform thing: sexual confidence. By seeking out those who have ample sexual experience, the younger party can experience a higher level of pleasure that many of their peers cannot provide yet. Plus, those who have been around the block a few times tend to know precisely what they're looking for in terms of a sexual encounter; there's not much guesswork to making an older partner sexually happy, which can lead to a more relaxing time for both parties.

glasses fetish

An extreme attraction to people wearing glasses. This rarely encompasses attraction to the glasses themselves, though that is possible.

glory hole

A hole in a wall or other dividing object through which people can perform anonymous sex acts, typically by one person inserting a penis or phallic object through the hole from one side and another person inserting it into themself on the other side. Glory holes are often found in public places, and are typically meant to be secretive, though some adult stores and other places advertise glory holes.

glove fetish
An extreme attraction to gloves or to someone wearing gloves.

gokkun
A sexual act where one drinks the seminal fluid of one or more people.

golden screw
A sex act in which one releases urine instead of ejaculate upon orgasm.

golden shower
A fetishist sexual act in which one partner urinates on another. People who love golden showers typically are either urophiliacs (see urophilia, page 213) or have a power/control fetish.

gooning
The term for when one has been edging (see page 56) for a long time and finally reaches a point where holding back an orgasm is impossible. It is said that during a gooning phase, the person can focus on nothing but physical release, resulting in blank or distorted facial expressions.

gray asexuality
The space between sexuality and asexuality (see page 23), in which a person experiences only a very limited amount of sexual feeling.

greet and meat
A slang term for having sex with someone immediately after meeting them for the first time.

grinding
Similar to dry humping (see page 53), grinding is when two or more partners rub their bodies, specifically their genitals, against one another. Participants are often, but not always, clothed, and this is more a type of foreplay than it is a sex act meant to inspire orgasm.

group grope
A slang term for an orgy.

group masturbation
The term for three or more partners masturbating themselves in the same room or area.

group sex
Any sexual act that involves more than two partners.

guybrator
A slang term for any sex toy that is meant to massage or

stimulate a prostate, penis, or testicles, such as a cock ring or harness.

gymnophilia
A fetish for nudity, whether being nude or seeing one's partner nude.

H

---

hamartophilia
A fetish for "going against the rules"—breaking the law, going against a religious code, or general wrongdoing.

hand job
A masturbatory sex act where hands are used to stimulate one's own or a partner's genitals.

hanky code
The hanky code is a system for finding anonymous, typically queer sex. Different colored handkerchiefs designate sex acts that one is willing to perform. By wearing a handkerchief on a certain position on one's body (on the right or left wrist, in a back pocket, etc.), people can advertise their preferences and match up with those who like the same things.

Developed in the 1970s, the hanky code was an effective method of finding a gay or lesbian sexual partner for those who had to keep their sexual preferences secret. While it's not the best way to find partners in today's world of sex and dating apps, where anyone can specify exactly what they're into and browse partners accordingly, it's still an interesting part of LGBT history. Each color of handkerchief had a specific kind of act associated with it, and each place the handkerchief could be tied to on the body was associated with the kinds of roles one would take on in those acts. For example, a light blue handkerchief, signaling the request for oral sex, could be worn on the right wrist to signal that they are a giving partner. If worn on the left wrist, it would mean they'd like to be a receiving partner.

happy baby position
A penetrative sex position in which the receiving partner lies on their back, with their knees bent up towards their chest and touching their shoulders if possible. This position makes penetration extremely easy, especially vaginal penetration.

happy ending
This refers to when any typically nonsexual act winds up (accidentally or otherwise) becoming sexual or causes someone to achieve orgasm. This is often used in reference to a "happy ending massage," where patrons pay masseuses at erotic parlors to give them hand or blow jobs at the end of their massage.

haptephilia
A condition that causes one to experience extreme arousal from being touched. Unlike non-haptephiliacs, who typically need stimulation of an erogenous zone in order to achieve sexual satisfaction, haptephiliacs feel sexually aroused when touched anywhere on their body, such as the back of their hand, their elbow, or their foot.

hard-on
A slang term for an erect penis.

hard swap
A term used in the swinging (see page 198) community for situations in which two or more couples are swinging and give full permission to do any sexual act, including penetrative sex. Also called a "full swap."

harmatophilia
A fetish for people who break rules. Harmatophiliacs would really love to be with a hamartophiliac (see hamartophilia, page 74).

head rest position
An oral sex position in which both partners lie on their sides, head to toe. The receiving partner moves their top leg behind their bottom leg, creating a space on the bottom leg where the giving partner can rest their head while giving oral sex.

heavy petting
The term for any foreplay or pre-penetrative sex act that includes caressing, fondling, or kissing the body.

hematolagnia
Also known as a blood fetish, this fetish causes fetishists to be aroused by the sight, smell, taste, or presence of blood. Blood fetishists often participate in acts of bloodletting, either of themselves or their partners (see blood play, page 31; also see vampirism, page 217).

heterosexual
A person who experiences sexual attraction to someone of an opposing gender. This typically refers to attraction between males and females.

hickey
A bruise that appears on the skin from a sexual bite. These reddish-purple marks are caused by prolonged suction, so not every sexual bite will lead to a hickey.

Hickeys—the bane of the sneaky sexual teenager or adult. A clear sign of sexual activity, these marks can be tricky to hide, and the only true way to get rid of them is to wait for them to go away on their own. However, that hasn't stopped people from trying some odd methods to get rid of these telling spots, including rubbing toothbrushes, hairbrushes, or coins on the area; slathering them with toothpaste or pieces of potatoes; or eating a large quantity of strawberries (a fruit with a high amount of salicylic acid, which helps promote blood flow). If you do find yourself with a hickey that you need to hide or hasten away, one of the best ways to help the healing process is to apply ice or a cold compress. This helps reduce swelling in the area. Applying a lotion or cream containing vitamin K to the area will also help; you can find it at most pharmacies. Vitamin K promotes healthy blood flow in the skin; it's a vitamin commonly found in leafy greens and dark vegetables, though eating a bunch of spinach won't make your hickey go away quickly.

---

hierophilia

A fetish for objects, places, and people associated with one's chosen religion. Hierophiliacs may experience arousal in churches or temples or on "holy" sites, or may want to masturbate with religious paraphernalia. Some even experience arousal when saying a prayer or when reading a religious text.

hirsutophilia

A fetish for the sight or feeling of hair, including hair on the head, armpits, genitals, or elsewhere. Most hirsutophiliacs have an attraction to human hair, but this fetish can also include fur (see doraphilia, page 52).

hodophilia

A feeling of sexual arousal experienced by traveling to

or discovering new places. Those with hodophilia love to explore and travel to new places, but will likely not experience the same arousal when traveling somewhere they already know.

homosexual
A person who experiences sexual attraction to people of the same gender. This typically refers to attraction of men to men or women to women.

horny
A slang term for feeling sexually aroused and wanting to participate in some type of sexual activity.

hotdogging
A slang term for an ass job (see page 23).

hybristophilia
A sexual attraction to dangerous criminals, specifically ones that have committed acts of rape, murder, or other capital offenses.

A startling trend has been on the rise for the past few decades—more and more people are coming out as hybristophiliacs, announcing their love for serial killers and those who participate in genocides or other killings. Though this trend extends to all genders, hybristophiliacs today are most commonly women, ranging in age from very young to very old, but all attracted to those people (typically male) who perpetrate violence. Whether this is a new trend or just one that has become more apparent with the expanse of media dedicated to crime and death, we don't really know. The causes of this fetish are being studied intensively. Some theorize that it has to do with the act of killing itself, making it more of a death fantasy; others believe it is a control fetish, or a belief that one can change someone for the better. Some scientists even believe it to be an evolutionary trait, theorizing that those who kill wantonly could be subconsciously seen as more protective of potential children, even though the risk of them killing said offspring is greater than average. Unfortunately, vocal hybristophiliacs are often judged to be as morally inept as those who actually commit the crimes, even though studies seem to show that the attraction is purely sexual and that most hybristophiliacs have no interest in killing.

hygrophilia
A fetish for bodily fluids or excretions, such as tears, semen, vaginal discharge, feces, or sweat.

hymen
A thin membrane that stretches around the vaginal opening.

Many people believe that those with vaginas who have sex for the first time will (or should) experience hymen breakage. However, this is not supposed to happen; the hymen is not a barrier to the vagina, like the seal on a yogurt container. Rather, it consists of fringed bits of skin that circle the outside opening of the vagina, and it is just another part of the organ. Sometimes it does stretch all the way across the vaginal opening, but typically it does not. It can tear during sexual intercourse, and this can hurt and cause bleeding, but it takes a lot of pressure for this to happen. The bleeding and pain typically associated with losing one's virginity are likely due to forcefulness, lack of lubrication, or not being relaxed, which can cause the body to tense up. (Because of the myth that those with vaginas always feel pain with their first penetrative experience, most of them come to expect it). And of course, the stigma around not bleeding or not feeling pain can make people feel guilty or that they've done something wrong, when the truth is that the experience will be different for everyone.

---

hyper fetish
An attraction to those with abnormally large body parts. This fetish is usually associated with genitals or sexual body parts such as large breasts, but it can extend to any part of the body. Those with a hyper fetish will often surgically augment their bodies or the bodies of their partners to achieve an exaggerated size.

hypersexuality
A sexual condition that causes one to experience much more sexual desire than the average person. Hypersexuals are not necessarily sex addicts, but they constantly experience arousal.

You may have heard of the colloquial names for hyper-sexuality: nymphomania, which applies hypersexuality to those who are female, and satyriasis, which applies to those who are male. These terms take their names respectively from the old Greek myths about nymphs and satyrs, creatures whose amorous nature would often butt heads with the more chaste human population.

hypophilia

A sexual condition that causes one to experience sexual desire much less often than the average person. Those with this condition have sex very infrequently, but still do experience arousal and desire. Hypophilia can develop when someone is having physical stimulation issues, such as impotence (see page 83), or in times of great stress. In these cases, it is possible to find a medical solution to hypophilia.

I

icolagnia
A fetish for nudity in art and media; things like statues, photos, paintings, or pornographic videos will interest those with icolagnia.

impact play
A BDSM term for striking someone or being struck for sexual satisfaction. This can include spanking, flogging, whipping, caning, and many other activities. A large part of impact play is seeing the physical manifestation of the impact; for example, as a bruise or scrape.

impotence
A sexual condition that causes those with penises to be unable to maintain an erection.

Also known as erectile dysfunction, impotence is a leading cause of sexual frustration for many sexually active people. There are many causes of impotence, including things like diabetes and heart disease; however, it should be noted that it is most often caused by bodily impairment or stress, and a good portion of people with penises will experience some form of impotence in their life. The situation can easily be treated medically, and there is absolutely no shame in getting such treatment. After all, it's better to get help getting up than to feel down about...well, being down.

incest
The term for sexual activity between immediate family members.

infidelity
The term for violation of trust in a sexual or romantic relationship. When this trust is broken in those who are married, it is called adultery (see page 10).

inflatophilia
A fetish for inflatable objects, such as inflatable dolls or balloons. (Also see balloon fetish, page 28).

J

Jack-and-Jill-Off party
A type of non-penetrative orgy in which multiple partners will masturbate themselves in the same room or area. The mix is usually male and female; an all-male party is known as a Jack-Off party, and an all-female party is known as a Jill-Off party.

jackhammering
A sex act in which a partner penetrates an orifice with a penis or sexual object in a very fast, repetitive manner.

jerking off
A slang term for masturbation, usually used for those with penises.

jilling off
A slang term for masturbation, usually used for those with vaginas.

jizz
A slang term for semen (see page 167).

job
In sexual terms, a "job" is a sex act in which genitals are masturbated with a partner's body part. A hand job (see page 74), of course, uses hands, and a blow job (see page 31) uses a partner's mouth, but any body part can be used.

john
The term sex workers use to refer to their customers to keep them anonymous.

johnson
A slang term for a penis.

joygasm
A slang term for experiencing sexual gratification from accomplishing a challenging feat or act. This is extremely subjective, as everyone considers different things to be challenging.

Sexual terms and slang are constantly being invented and changed, but there is no greater way than media to spread new words into the mainstream. The word *joygasm* first appeared in the movie *Batman Forever*: The Riddler exclaims it when destroying Batman's cave. Terms like "Netflix and chill" originated on social media, the word *fembot* (see page 62) originated in an episode of *The Bionic Woman*, and *Austin Powers* gave us words like *shaggable*. Also, though not one hundred percent proven, the popular acronym MILF (Mothers I'd Like to Fuck) seems to have originated from the movie *American Pie*.

---

just the tip
A slang term for inserting only the head of the penis into an orifice (typically a vagina).

K

Kama Sutra
The Kama Sutra is an ancient text from India that details human sexuality.

Though most people know it as a guide for new and often difficult sexual positions, the original Kama Sutra primarily discusses the philosophy of sex and its relationship to love and morality in one's life. The goal of the book is to balance physical and mental desire within the reader. Though the original text was intended strictly for heterosexual men, many Western translations of the book expand its teachings to all genders and sexualities.

karada
A BDSM sex toy, also known as a rope web. The karada is used to bind a submissive's entire body by wrapping them in an intricate and weblike pattern of rope.

karezza
A sex act in which a giving partner will resist orgasming during penetrative sex and will end the sex act without physical release. Karezza is often practiced in Taoist circles as a way to emphasize the intimacy of sex instead of focusing on the orgasm.

katoptronophilia
A fetish for mirrors, including looking at oneself or a partner in a mirror or having sex in front of a mirror.

key party
A type of party specific to the swinging (see page 198) community, at which one partner of a married couple will place their keys in a bowl. Once each couple has put keys into the bowl, the other partners will then pick a set of keys out of the bowl and leave with the person whose keys they picked.

kinesophilia
A fetish for movement or exercise—one's own or a partner's—including workouts like running, spinning, or any kind of cardio routine.

kleptophilia
A fetish for stealing or for watching things be stolen.

klismaphilia
A fetish for the injection of liquid into one's anus, typically achieved through an enema.

klittra
A slang term for masturbation involving the vagina or clitoris. The term was developed in 2014 in Sweden, when the Swedish Association for Sexuality Education realized there was no good word to describe clitoral or vaginal masturbation and decided to crowdsource a new word.

kneel and sit position
A penetrative sex position in which the giving partner kneels down on a bed or other surface, and the receiving partner lowers themself onto the giving partner. This allows the receiving partner to control movement.

knismolagnia
A fetish for being tickled or for watching someone else be tickled. Foot and armpit fetishes are often associated with knismolagnia, because those areas tend to be much more sensitive to tickling than many other parts of the body.

L

labia

A part of the vulva; the outer lips that surround the vagina. The labia can be extremely sensitive and very receptive to sexual stimulation.

The labia are actually made up of two parts—the labia majora and the labia minora. The labia majora are the outermost folds, and the part that is readily visible when looking at the vulva. Besides the pubic bone, pubic hairs are most commonly found on the outside of the labia majora. The labia minora are the inner layer of folds, though don't be fooled by the name: the labia minora isn't necessarily smaller in size than the labia majora. Some people have the same size for both, or even a bigger labia minora; it's not unusual and it doesn't make a difference for the body. Both parts of the labia are tasked with protecting the vagina, clitoris, and urethra from dirt and other things that can cause harm to these parts.

lace fetish
A fetish for wearing, feeling, or seeing lace, either on clothing or by itself. Because lace is typically seen as a "feminine" object, many crossdressers fetishize it as a symbol of womanhood.

lactophilia
The technical term for a fetish for adult breastfeeding (see page 9).

lady boner
A slang term for sexual excitement by someone who identifies as female.

Lady Godiva position
An oral sex position specifically meant for cunnilingus. The giving partner lies down with their head touching a headboard, wall, or other hard object. The receiving partner then straddles the giving partner's head with their knees and lowers themself onto their partner's mouth while holding onto the headboard. This allows the receiving partner to lower and raise themself at will and gives the giving partner easier access to the labia and clitoris.

leptosadism
The term for experiencing arousal from inflicting a small amount of pain on a partner. This is not as intense as sadism, but meant more as teasing and an act of power over a partner.

lesbian

The term for someone who identifies as female who is strictly attracted to other women.

lesbophilia

A fetish for lesbians and seeing acts of lesbianism. This fetish is typically held by heterosexual males.

LGBT

The acronym for Lesbian, Gay, Bisexual, and Transgender. "LGBT" is a blanket term for any sexuality or gender that is considered to be "outside the norm." The letters are often expanded to include Q for Queer (see page 148), I for Intersex (the term for someone who was born with genitals that are not considered "typical" for their gender or genitals that fall somewhere between the male and female norm), and/or A for Asexual (see page 23).

libido

Also known as the sex drive, *libido* is the scientific term for the amount of sexual desire one experiences. Everyone's libido is different, and it can change at any time due to outside factors, such as medication or life events.

lingerie

Elegant underclothing, such as bras or panties, that is made to attract or excite a sexual partner. Lingerie is usually made of more exotic materials than regular underwear, such as silk or lace.

Little Dipper position
A penetrative sex position in which the giving partner lies on the floor between two pieces of low furniture (such as a couch and a chair). The receiving partner puts their hands on one piece of furniture and their legs on the other and lowers themself onto the giving partner, inserting the giving partner into themself.

lotus blossom position
A penetrative sex position in which the giving partner sits on a surface with their legs crossed. The receiving partner then straddles the giving partner and initiates penetration. Also called the lotus position.

M

macrogenitalism

1. A fetish for those with genitals that are significantly larger than average.

2. The sexual condition of having larger-than-average genitalia.

macrophilia

A sexual attraction to giants and those with gigantism (people who experience excessive growth or height). Macrophiliacs' attraction specifically centers around those who are very tall, as opposed to those who are very heavy.

Magic Mountain position

An anal sex position in which the receiving partner lies facedown on a pile of pillows or another object so that their bottom end is elevated and their head is on the floor or other surface. The giving partner penetrates the receiving partner from behind.

maiesiophilia
The fetish for pregnancy, whether for being pregnant or for seeing one's partner pregnant.

make-up sex
A slang term for sexual intercourse that takes place after an argument. It is often used as a way to build bonds of love and clear away negative feelings from a disagreement.

manual sex
Any sex act that is done with ones hands or fingers, either on oneself or a partner.

maschalagnia
A fetish for armpits, including touching, smelling, licking, or seeing one's own or a partner's armpit. Often associated with hirsutophilia (see page 78) and knismolagnia (see page 90).

masochism
The act of experiencing pleasure by having pain inflicted upon oneself.

mastigothyma
A fetish for being flogged. This fetish is specific to the

person receiving the flogging and does not apply to watching others being flogged.

Master

A name for a dominant partner in a Master/slave relationship, a type of BDSM relationship that involves strict control. The Master/slave relationship goes even further than a typical dominant/submissive relationship; Masters are always in control of their slaves in sexual, social, and domestic situations. This type of relationship is always negotiated and consensual.

masturbation

The stimulation of one's own genitals, either with one's hands, an adult toy, or another assisting object.

mechanophilia

A sexual attraction to machines, such as cars, computers, and other electronic, professional, or household machinery.

medical fetish

A general term for any fetish for a person or object related to the medical field: doctors, nurses, hospitals, stethoscopes, thermometers, and so on.

melissophilia

A fetish for bees, wasps, or any insect with a stinger. This is a type of entomophilia (see page 57).

melolagnia

A fetish for music—either playing music or hearing music. With melolagnia, arousal is caused by the melodies, and not by suggestive lyrics.

merinthophilia

A fetish for being tied, bound, or otherwise physically restricted. This fetish is often associated with power play, in which the bound person relishes giving control over to another person.

microphilia

A fetish or sexual preference for partners who are significantly smaller or shorter than oneself.

mile high club

The slang term for having sex while in an airplane, helicopter, or other aircraft.

missionary position

The most well-known penetrative sex position. The receiving partner lies on their back with their legs spread, and the giving partner lies on top of the receiving partner and initiates penetration.

No one knows for sure why or how the missionary position got its name. A popular story states that during the

colonial era when Christian missionaries visited possible converts in Africa, Polynesia, and other foreign places, they would witness public sex in many different positions, which astonished them. They chastised the locals for their sexual customs and instead encouraged them to use the more "godly" method of procreation, face-to-face with a man on top and a woman on her back, which then became known as the missionary position. There's no real evidence that this story is true, but it was held in such fascinating esteem with popular media of the 1970s that the name became a true part of the sexual lexicon.

---

mixophilia
The fetish for seeing sex acts performed, either on video or live.

money shot
A term used in pornography to describe male ejaculation onto a partner's face, chest, or genitals.

morphophilia
A general fetish for body types that exist outside of the "normal" spectrum, such as those with dwarfism or gigantism, those who are obese, or those who were born without certain limbs. Most people who experience morphophilia can also be grouped into a specific fetish for the type of body they are attracted to; it is rare that a morphophiliac is attracted to all types of unusual bodies.

muff diving
A slang term for cunnilingus.

mummification
A very advanced bondage act, in which the submissive is bound head to toe with things like plastic wrap, tarps, a body bag, bandages, or other types of coverings, leaving the person completely immobilized.

*Note: wrapping the nose and/or mouth can cause someone to not be able to breathe, which can lead to fainting or death. If you decide to participate in mummification, please make sure that adequate breathing spaces are provided for the wrapped person.

munch
A gathering of people who are interested in BDSM.

munching
A slang term for cunnilingus.

mustache ride
An oral sex position in which a receiving partner sits on the face of a giving partner with a mustache.

mysophilia
A fetish for filth, or for being or feeling physically dirty. Mysophiliacs enjoy smelling foul and will often abstain from bathing or changing clothes for long periods of time.

N

nailing
A slang term for having sex with someone, typically in reference to a giving partner having sex with a specific receiving partner.

narratophilia
A fetish for words and language that have to do with sex. Narratophiliacs often experience intense arousal when telling sex stories to their partners or when listening to sex stories.

nasolingus
A sex act in which one licks or sucks a partner's nose or nostrils.

nasophilia
A fetish for noses, possibly including the intense desire to penetrate a partner's nostrils.

negotiation
A BDSM term for the important conversation between participants entering into a dominant/submissive relationship to determine each partner's sexual preferences and limits. This also serves as the point at which both parties will (verbally or otherwise) consent to the sex acts within their relationship.

nirvana position
A penetrative sex position that is a variation on the missionary position (see page 98). In the nirvana position, the receiving partner will lie on their back, but instead of spreading their legs, they will keep their legs close together and stretch their arms above their head. This position leads to better clitoral stimulation for receiving partners with vaginas.

nookie
A slang term for sex.

nooner
A slang term for sex that takes place during the early afternoon or on a lunch break from work.

normophilia
A fetish for laws, religious rules, and traditions that are considered "normal." This typically includes heteronormative ideals and conservative thinking.

NSA

An acronym for "no strings attached," a type of relationship that is strictly sexual in nature, where neither partner feels or develops romantic attraction.

nyctophilia

A fetish or sexual preference for darkness or nighttime. Nyctophiliacs may prefer to have sex with the lights off, or may like to be blindfolded during sex.

O

O face
A slang term to describe the often distorted facial expression one makes while experiencing orgasm.

objectophilia
A fetish for inanimate objects. Objectophiliacs will often seek out objects that meet certain qualifications; they may be attracted to round objects, or objects of a certain color, or ones that have a specific purpose.

object sexuality
Like objectophiliacs, objectum sexuals experience sexual attraction to inanimate objects, but their lust is directed towards one or two specific objects, such as one specific chair, or in the case of one objectum sexual woman, the Eiffel Tower. Objectum sexuals typically feel a romantic connection to their chosen object as well.

oculophilia
A fetish for eyes. This can be an attraction to a particular color or shape of eye, or even to the particular placement of the eyes on a partner's face.

odaxelagnia
A fetish for being bitten or for biting someone. This can involve bites anywhere on the body, and is not limited specifically to erogenous zones.

odontophilia
A fetish for teeth, including feeling teeth on one's body, licking a partner's teeth, looking at a toothy smile, or holding a tooth. Odontophiliacs may also like being bitten (see odaxelagnia, previous definition).

olfactophilia
A fetish for certain smells, particularly the smell of a partner's body. The arousal tends to be intensified when the smell comes from a partner's genitals or through their sweat.

omniromantic
A person who can experience feelings of romantic love for all genders and sexualities.

omnisexual
Someone who can experience sexual attraction to those of every gender and sexuality type.

one-column tie
A type of BDSM bondage knot meant to bind an appendage to an outside object, like a leg to a chair or an arm to a headboard.

one-night stand
A one-time sexual encounter with an individual, typically involving anonymous sex (see page 20).

open relationship
A sexual and/or romantic relationship between two or more partners in which each partner is allowed to have sexual relations with others outside of the relationship.

open swinging
A type of swinging (see page 198) where swingers will swap partners and have sex with those temporary partners while everyone is in the same room.

OPP
Acronym for "one-penis policy," a type of open relationship (see page 106) that involves one male partner and multiple female partners.

oral servitude
A BDSM term for when a submissive is made to perform oral sex on their dominant partner for extended periods of time.

oral sex simulator

1. A sex toy designed for those with vaginas and clitorises that utilizes suction to simulate cunnilingus.

2. A sex toy designed for those with penises that is molded to be just like a person's mouth.

ORE

An acronym for "old relationship energy," a term used to describe feelings of stability in a long-term romantic or sexual relationship.

orgasm

The apex of intense sexual pleasure that typically happens while participating in a sex act. This feeling triggers a response in the body that causes those with penises to release ejaculate (see page 56) and causes vaginal contractions in those with vaginas. Partners of any gender may experience muscular contractions, and most will experience a calming of their sexual desire afterward.

orgasm control

A sexual practice in which one holds oneself in a state of high sexual arousal for an extended period of time without orgasming. Orgasm control is said to make the eventual orgasm much more intense than normal.

orgasm denial
A sex act often performed in BDSM circles, in which a dominant partner will keep a submissive partner in a high state of arousal for an extended period of time, not granting the submissive permission to orgasm until the dominant allows it.

orgasm gap
In sexology (see page 174), the term for the difference in the number of orgasms each gender achieves on average. Among those in heterosexual relationships, men are likely to have three orgasms for every one orgasm a woman has. For women in lesbian relationships, the orgasm gap is much smaller.

orgy
A party or gathering where all guests are encouraged to openly perform any sexual act with any other consenting guest or guests.

Orgies have always had their place in human history. The Romans were said to have had lavish parties where food, wine, and prostitutes were freely available; the Egyptians had annual parties dedicated to the goddess Sekhmet where whole groups of people would get extremely drunk and have sex with each other in public. Just about every culture has a history of group sex. But in 2006, a group of people in Japan actually set the world record for the biggest orgy ever recorded! The event was called "500

Person Sex," and as the name states, the orgy featured five hundred people all having sex at the same time in one room. The event was choreographed, so all of the couples moved in tandem. The filmed event was also released on a DVD which is available for purchase, making it not only the biggest orgy, but one of the largest scale pornography films ever made.

---

orientation play

A sex act in which someone engages in sexual activity with a partner of a different orientation from their own. For example, a heterosexual man might seek out another man for orientation play, or a gay man might engage a woman.

OSO

An acronym for "other significant other," a term used in the polyamorous community to signify one's partner's other partner.

OTK

An acronym for "over the knee," which refers to when a submissive is bent over a dominant's knee to be spanked.

outcall

The term for when a sex worker travels to the location of a john or client.

outdoor bondage
A BDSM term for restraining a submissive in a public place—for example, tying a submissive to a bike rack, streetlamp, or park bench.

overpass position
A penetrative sex position in which the receiving partner starts by lying on the ground, then lifts their legs into the air and over their head in a shoulder stand, exposing their genital orifices. The giving partner then stands over the receiving partner, one foot by the receiving partner's shoulder on the ground, the other by the receiving partner's back. The giving partner initiates penetration and thrusts in a squatting motion.

ownership
A BDSM term for when a dominant partner assumes complete control over a submissive partner. The submissive partner is still free to leave the relationship at any time, but while an active participant, the entirety of their life is directed by their owner.

P

P-spot
An erogenous zone found in those with prostates. The P-spot is located about two or three inches inside of the rectum, though the location is different for every individual.

pack-and-play dildo
A phallic sex toy that is soft enough to be "packed" into someone's pants, giving the appearance of having a penis, but also rigid enough for penetration.

packing
Using a toy or other object to simulate having a penis.

padding
A role-playing (see page 156) fetish practice in which layers of clothing or other materials are added to a partner's body to simulate weight gain.

paddle
A BDSM sex toy. Typically made of wood, a paddle consists of a flat, wide surface connected to a handle and is used to administer spankings.

paddling
The BDSM sex act of repeatedly spanking a submissive partner. This is typically done with a paddle, but any similar object may be used.

padlock position
A penetrative sex position in which the receiving partner sits with spread legs on the edge of a piece of furniture that is about waist height for the giving partner (such as a table or countertop). The giving partner then inserts themselves into the receiving partner, and the receiving partner wraps their legs around the giving partner.

pain play
The sadomasochistic term (see sadomasochism, page 160) for sex acts that incorporate pain. Also referred to as S&M or torture, pain play involves both mental and physical pain, inflicted in a way that has been consensually agreed upon by all partners involved.

pain slut
A slang term for a person, typically a masochist, who enjoys receiving tremendous amounts of pain during sexual activity.

painal
A slang term for any anal sex act which causes pain, either intentionally or not, to either partner.

paingasm
An orgasm that is caused by pain stimulation.

panel gag
A BDSM sex toy; a ball gag (see page 27) that has a piece of fabric or leather, known as a "panel," covering the front of the ball. The panel holds the ball in place and effectively covers the entire mouth.

panic snap
A type of fastener used on BDSM binding devices that allows for the immediate release of the binding. They can be used to quickly release a submissive in emergencies, or if a submissive ever feels uncomfortable.

panromantic
Someone who feels romantic attraction to all types of people, regardless of gender or sexuality.

pansexual
Someone who feels sexual attraction to all types of people, regardless of gender or sexuality.

panty fetish
A fetish for panties, particularly when they are used or soiled.

panty play
The incorporation of panties into any sexual activity.

pantyhose fetish
A fetish for pantyhose; in particular, the feeling of wearing pantyhose, or watching a partner put on, wear, or remove pantyhose.

parachute
A BDSM sex toy used in CBT (see page 38); a small collar, typically made of leather, which is placed around the scrotum. Four long chains hang from the bottom of the parachute, weighing the collar down. Additional weights can be attached to the ends of the chains.

parallel play
When two or more couples have sex in the same room. This is different from an orgy (see page 108) in that coupled partners have sex with each other only and are not free to have sex with the others in the room.

parallel polyamory
A polyamorous relationship (see polyamory, page 128) where one person will have relationships with two or

more other people, but those others are not involved with each other, as friends, acquaintances, or otherwise. For example, if Alice is married to Ben, but is also dating Chris, Ben and Chris do not have any kind of relationship. Alice, Ben, and Chris are practicing parallel polyamory.

paramour
1. A term for a non-married or outside member of a poly-amorous relationship.

2. A sophisticated term for "lover."

paraphilia
Any sexual condition in which a person's arousal is contingent on something that is dangerous, illegal, socially unacceptable, or has a negative effect on their physical or mental health.

pareunia
A medical term for sexual intercourse.

partialism
The term for a fetish for one particular part of the body. For example, a foot fetish (see page 65) is a type of partialism.

parting the red sea
A slang term for performing cunnilingus on a partner who is on their period.

115

PassionSkin
A type of thermoplastic elastomer (see page 204) that is well known for its use in sex toy production. PassionSkin closely imitates the feel of real human skin, and so it is used to cover many kinds of dildos, fleshlights, and other such toys.

pay 4 play
A slang term for any situation where one pays for sexual activities.

pearl necklace
A sex act in which someone with a penis ejaculates onto a partner's neck or upper chest.

pearl tramp stamp
A sex act in which someone with a penis ejaculates onto a partner's lower back.

pearly gates position
A sex position where the giving partner will lie flat on their back and the receiving partner will lie faceup on top of them (both partners will be looking up at the ceiling). From here, the partners can engage in penetration or masturbation.

pecattiphilia
A fetish for doing things that one believes to be sinful. What

qualifies as "sinful" is entirely subjective, but examples could include sodomy, incest, or simply extramarital sex.

pecker
A slang term for a penis.

peepshow position
An oral sex position where both partners lie on their sides, with the giving partner's head down by the receiving partner's crotch. The receiving partner opens their legs, allowing the giving partner to begin fellatio or cunnilingus.

pegging
A sex act in which one wears a strap-on (see page 195) to penetrate a partner anally.

penile dysmorphia
A sexual condition that causes the sufferer to believe their penis is not big enough to satisfy a partner sexually.

penile prosthesis
An implant used as a treatment for erectile dysfunction (see impotence, page 83). It is inserted into the penis to assist with blood flow and retention.

penis
A reproductive sex organ with a head, a shaft, and a

urethra through which urine and semen pass through and exit the body. The penis becomes engorged with blood during arousal, causing it to stiffen; this is called an erection (see page 57) and makes it easier for those with penises to penetrate their partners.

penis cage
A BDSM sex toy; a tube-like cage that is locked around the penis to prevent direct stimulation of the organ.

penis humiliation
The act, often practiced in BDSM, of belittling the qualities of a partner's penis, including shape, size, sexual effectiveness, color, or firmness.

penis limiter
A sex toy worn on a penis which serves to limit how deeply it can penetrate a partner.

penis pump
A device, consisting of a cylinder connected to an electronic or hand pump, meant to temporarily ease the effects of impotence (see page 83). The cylinder is placed over the penis, creating a partial vacuum. Using the pump increases the vacuum pressure, causing blood pressure in the penis to rise. This results in a temporary erection, which can be held in place by putting a ring or band at the base of the penis.

pedovestism
A fetish for dressing like a young child.

perineum
The erogenous zone located between the anus and the sex organs. In slang terms, this area is known as the taint.

perineum massager
A small sex toy meant to stimulate the perineum through vibration. This can cause increased arousal and more intense orgasms.

period play/period sex
The fetish for or act of having sex while either oneself or a partner is having their period.

permaboner
An erection that lasts longer than average. Permaboners that last for more than a few hours can be exceedingly painful.

persistent sexual arousal syndrome
A sexual condition, usually abbreviated as PSAS, that causes a person to become excessively physically aroused at random, resulting in an almost continual state of arousal. This physical state of arousal is not connected to one's mental state, but sexual activity can relieve the tension of people with PSAS.

personal massager
A term for any vibrating sex toy, particularly ones that are not phallic in shape. These toys are intended for masturbation, but they are also often used as full-body massagers.

perversion
A term for any sexual behavior that is considered immoral or abhorrent.

pervertable
Any object that can be used as a sex toy or incorporated into sexual activities—for example, a cucumber that can be inserted into a vagina for masturbation.

pescatarian porn
A slang term for pornography in which the only nude participants are people with vaginas.

petticoating
A form of humiliation in which a male submissive is made to wear a frilly petticoat. Those who enjoy this activity are said to have a petticoat fetish.

phallophilia
A fetish for large penises, either in length or width.

pheromones
Chemicals emitted from the body that can affect the

behavior of others who come in contact with them. Sexual pheromones can help attract a mate who would be compatible for reproductive purposes, and they can also cause alarm or a change in sexual desire in potential partners.

philanderer
A term for someone in a relationship who has sex outside of the relationship.

philemaphobia
The fear of kissing. Philemaphobics may be afraid of germs or contracting viruses, or may be averse to the physical sensation of kissing.

phobophilia
A fetish for feeling afraid. Phobophiliacs tend to focus on the emotional aspects of fear, rather than the physical; for example, most phobophiliacs would enjoy thinking about being chased or threatened, but might not like to have a knife pressed against them.

phone operator
The term for a sex worker who works for a paid phone-sex company.

phone sex
A sex act in which erotic words and phrases are exchanged in a phone conversation. Parties on both ends of the

conversation may masturbate while listening to their partner speak.

phygephilia
A fetish for living as a fugitive or for being on the run.

physical humiliation
A BDSM sexual practice in which a submissive consents to being made to do degrading activities, having intense restrictions placed on them, or being constantly mocked or told they are bad.

pictophilia
The technical term for pornography addiction. Pictophiliacs are consumed by an intense need to view erotic materials, fetishizing them as preferable to partnered sex.

pie in the sky position
A cunnilingus position in which the partner with a vagina lies on their back and lifts their legs up and over their head, or as far back as they can go. This exposes the vagina and allows the giving partner easier access to the genitals.

piggy play
A term used in the gay community to refer to kink or BDSM.

piledriver position
A penetrative sex position in which the receiving partner lies on their back and lifts their legs up and over their head (or as far as they can go). The giving partner then stands over the receiving partner's crotch, and, facing the receiving partner, initiates penetration. This is similar to the overpass position (see page 110) except that the giving partner stands facing the receiving partner instead of perpendicular to them.

pillory bed
A bed used in BDSM play. Pillory beds have a stock (just like the ones you see in depictions of medieval times) built into the headboard so submissives can be held in place for bedded sexual activities.

pillow princess/pillow queen
A slang term for someone who enjoys receiving sexual pleasure but does not intend to reciprocate or put effort into any sexual activities.

pimp
A pimp is a male agent for sex workers; female agents are called madams. Pimps procure new sex workers, market their "clients" to potential customers, and handle the money earned from customer interactions. (Note: While this is what pimps are supposed to do, it's not always what they actually do. Many pimps engage in trafficking people

into different countries, operating illegal sex work rings, and using psychological abuse to force people, especially young women, to make money for them).

pink taco
A slang term for vagina.

P-in-V sex
An abbreviation for "penis-in-vagina sex"; any penetrative sex that includes a penis entering a vagina.

pirate's bounty position
A sex position in which the receiving partner lies on their back with one leg flat on the ground and one leg on their partner's shoulder (forming a shape like a mast on a boat). The giving partner initiates penetration from a kneeling position.

pitcher
A slang term for a penetrating (giving) partner.

pitching a tent
A slang term for having an erection.

pity fuck
A term for engaging in sexual activity because one feels sorry for one's partner, or wants to make one's partner feel better.

plank on top position
A variation on the missionary position (see page 98) in which the giving partner stays in a push-up or plank position during intercourse. Also known as the hip raised plank position.

plaster cast fetish
A fetish for plaster casts. This can include seeing people wearing casts on their limbs, or wearing a cast oneself.

plastic panties
Undergarments made of PVC that stretch over the groin area.

plastic panties fetish
A fetish for plastic panties—wearing them or seeing others wear them.

plasticuffs
Plastic handcuffs that are cheap, durable, and disposable. These are a favorite item of the BDSM community.

play
Any kinky or otherwise odd sexual activity. "Play" can be added onto any noun to describe a sex act; for example, if you liked tape and wanted to incorporate it into your activities, you could call it "tape play."

play party
A BDSM orgy at which attendees participate in BDSM practices, such as whipping, binding, and domination/submission.

play piercing
The act of giving piercings for sexual pleasure instead of for aesthetic beauty. Piercings of this kind can be placed anywhere, but are most typically done on the genitals (such as the penis or labia) or the nipples.

play punishment
Often referred to as "funishment," this type of BDSM punishment is meant to be more of an introduction between potential new partners or BDSM friends. The pain is very light and often done in a teasing manner.

playing the skin flute
1. A slang phrase for fellatio (see page 62).

2. A slang term for masturbating a penis.

playroom
A room designed for BDSM acts. Technically, any room where BDSM activities take place can be considered a playroom.

plow position

A penetrative sex position in which the receiving partner leans over the edge of a bed so their upper chest and head are resting on the bed and places their forearms out in front of them. The giving partner lifts up the hips of the receiving partner and penetrates them from behind.

plumber position

An oral sex position in which the receiving partner is down on all fours, legs apart. The giving partner lies underneath them, puts their head between the receiving partner's knees, and initiates oral sex.

plushophilia

The fetish for stuffed animals, or "plushies." Plushophiles delight in the collection of plushies, as well as feeling them or using them during sexual activities. Many believe plush-ophilia is a type of anaclitism (see page 16), especially for plushophiles who had stuffed animals as children.

podophilia

A fetish for feet; a synonym for "foot fetish" (see page 65).

pogonophilia

A fetish for beards, including touching beards, smelling or kissing beards, or having partners with beards. This is a type of doraphilia (see page 52).

poles apart position
A penetrative sex position in which the giving partner will lie on their side, and the receiving partner will lie in front of them, facing the same direction but with their head by their partner's feet. The giving partner can then enter vaginally or anally.

poly mixed relationship
Also known as a poly/mono relationship, this type of relationship involves one monogamous partner and one polyamorous partner. The poly partner will have sexual relationships with other people and the monogamous partner will not.

polyamory
Literally translated as "many loves," polyamory is the practice of having multiple romantic or sexual relationships at one time. Polyamorous people tend to need sexual interactions with multiple people in order to achieve sexual happiness.

polyandry
The practice of being married to multiple male partners at one time.

polycule
A network of people who are connected through romantic or sexual relationships. "Polycule" is a handy way to

describe the connection between a polyamorous person's lovers.

polyfamily
A group of polyamorous people (see polyamory, page 128) who consider each other to be family. Polyfamilies typically live together, but not always.

polyfidelity
This term describes a polyamorous relationship where all members of the relationship are equal to each other and are expected to be faithful to everyone in the relationship (in other words, they should not have sex with someone outside of the group).

polyfuckery
A divisive term used in the polyamorous community to describe someone who presents as polyamorous, but seems to be using the identity as a way to have one-night stands or hook-ups with people instead of relationships.

polygamy
The practice of being married to more than one person at a time.

polygyny
The practice of being married to multiple female partners at one time.

polykoity
The term for having multiple sexual partners, either at one time or over the course of a lifetime.

polyromantic
Someone who is romantically attracted to several, but not all, genders or sexualities.

polysaturated
A polyamorous person who is not currently seeking new partners, due to already having the desired number of partners or not having time to form new relationships.

polysexual
Someone who is sexually attracted to several, but not all, genders or sexualities.

polytrothism
A polyamorous relationship where any and all partners are held in equal regard. For example, if a polyamorous person who practices polytrothism has a husband and a boyfriend, both receive equal time and are regarded as being of equal importance.

polyunsaturated
A polyamorous person who is currently seeking new sexual or romantic relationships.

pomoromantic
A person who experiences romantic attraction, but does not wish to label or define their feelings in a conventional way. For example, a pomoromantic man who is attracted to another man would not want to call himself a homosexual, preferring not to give a name to his attraction.

pony boy/pony girl
A person, typically a submissive in a BDSM relationship, who takes sexual pleasure in role-playing ponies or horses. This includes letting their dominant partner ride them, neighing, and wearing pony gear (see next definition).

pony gear
A catchall term for a variety of sex toys that allow people to role-play as ponies and horses. These include things like saddles, bridles, bits, metal shoes, and even butt plugs (see page 35) with horse tails attached to the end. Pony play is common in the BDSM and furry (see page 67) communities.

pootie
A slang term for vagina, vulva, clitoris, labia, etc.

popping the cherry
A slang term for losing one's virginity, particularly when the virgin is female.

porking
A slang term for having sex.

pornado
A portmanteau of "porn" and "tornado"; a slang term for the amount of Internet porn one typically consumes during masturbation due to the overwhelming number of pop-ups most porn sites use to generate revenue.

pornocchio
A portmanteau of "porn" and "Pinocchio"; a slang term for a person who lies about their porn-watching habits.

pornography
The depiction of sexual activity in some form of media, whether drawing, photography, film, prose, or games. Pornography is one of the biggest industries in the world. The word itself is often shortened to *porn* or *porno*.

position training
A BDSM sexual practice in which submissives in a new relationship are shown how to properly perform the desired sexual positions of their dominant partner. Submissives must memorize these moves and may be punished later for not enacting them correctly.

positional furniture
Any furniture that is used specifically and only for sexual activities.

post-coital phase
The period after sex during which the body is in "recovery." During this phase, the blood from an erect penis or engorged clitoris will flow back into the body, allowing physical arousal to subside.

post-coital tristesse
A feeling of sexual dissatisfaction that can occur a short time after intercourse, leading to sadness, anxiety, or agitation. In extreme cases, people may also become aggressive. This feeling typically occurs in men, though the reason for it is still unknown.

post-orgasm torture
The practice of touching sensitive areas (such as the head of the penis or the tip of the clitoris) after an orgasm, causing overwhelming sensation.

post-scene plunge
The feelings of depression, fear, disgust, or guilt that may come after participating in BDSM play. These feelings can be felt by either a dominant or a submissive, but typically happen to those who are new to the BDSM scene.

postillionage
The technical term for stimulation of the anus or rectum.

posture collar
A BDSM sex toy used to restrict movement of a submissive's neck; a high, rigid collar that goes around a person's neck and ends just under the chin, enforcing a chin-up position.

power exchange
The term for a relationship in which one person voluntarily gives control over to their partner. This is the basis for most BDSM relationships.

power exchange levels
The descriptive system of degrees of emotional involvement in a power exchange. There are five named levels of exchange: conditional compliance (meant for a one-time BDSM experience where control is given for one night or one act), restricted ongoing acquiescence (for a casual BDSM relationship without commitment), provisional submission (for a casual or semi-serious relationship where high levels of control are given), the covenant of dominance and submission (for a committed D/S relationship), and absolute ownership (for people in a committed D/S relationship where the dominant partner has complete control over the submissive).

power play
The term for giving one partner dominancy or submissive-
ness during a sexual encounter.

pre-ejaculate
Also known as pre-cum, this is the clear, viscous fluid that
can come out of the penis during the start of sexual arousal.
The fluid typically contains very low levels of sperm. Some
people with penises do not secrete pre-cum at all, or not
during every sexual experience. It varies by individual.

predicament bondage
A type of bondage in which the bound person is placed
in an uncomfortable or awkward position, or given a challenging task to perform while bound. This type of bondage
often includes a humiliation aspect, and punishment can
be inflicted on those who fail the task.

premature ejaculation
A sexual condition in which a person with a penis ejaculates more quickly than normal, due either to extreme
stimulation or to mental inhibitions. Most people with
penises will experience premature ejaculation occasion-
ally, but continued occurrences can be linked to more
serious disorders, and those who experience it often
should consult a doctor.

pretzel dip position

A penetrative sex position in which the receiving partner lies on their left side and lifts their left leg. The giving partner kneels on top of the receiving partner's right leg and wraps their left leg around their waist, allowing the giving partner to penetrate deeply from the side.

priapism

The scientific term for a sexual condition where an erect penis does not return to its flaccid state after sex, but instead stays erect for a prolonged period of time. This can cause nerve damage and other kinds of damage to the penile tissues and increases the likelihood of future erectile issues.

PRICK

An acronym for "Personal Responsibility, Informed Consensual Kink." PRICK is a BDSM sexual philosophy which emphasizes each individual's responsibility to gather consent from their partners, understand the risks involved with the sexual acts they choose to engage in, and learn and know their own limits and the limits of any person they have sex with.

primal play

A type of BDSM encounter that focuses on natural, rough, and unregulated sexual impulses. Dominant partners are encouraged to give into any feeling they experience, and typically use only their own body (hands, teeth, etc.) for domination. Primal play is commonly associated with animal play (see page 20).

primary

For a polyamorous person, the relationship with the highest degree of priority. This is typically the person that one is committed to.

Prince Albert

A penis piercing; specifically, a metal ball that is worn at the end of the penis.

You may be wondering why a genital piercing would be named after a British royal, but there's a very interesting legend around Prince Albert, the consort of Queen Victoria. Apparently, Albert was so well-endowed that his monarch bride was embarrassed to be seen with him in the tight dress pants of the time, as his member would be so thoroughly outlined in the fabric. In order to rectify this, he had his penis pierced with a small ring and hooks sewn onto the sides of his pants, so he could actually hook up his penis to the inside seam, causing it not to show (as much). Historians debate whether the prince actually had such a piercing, but these hook/ring combos, called dressing hooks, were a common practice at that time.

prison guard position
A penetrative sex position similar to the doggy style position (see page 51). This position has the receiving partner on all fours or bent over a piece of furniture or bed. The receiving partner puts their wrists behind their back, and the giving partner holds them while penetrating from behind.

prison scening
A type of role-play that involves scenes and roles associated with prisons (for example, role-playing as a guard and a prisoner, or having sex through metal bars).

prison strap
A BDSM sex toy made entirely of rigid leather, designed to slap a submissive's backside. It looks like one long strap of leather with a handle.

privates-to-privates
A type of erotic massage that involves rubbing one's genitals on one's partner, aiming to bring them to climax through that stimulation alone. This is commonly requested from sex workers.

probe
A type of small, conical dildo or vibrator. Probes are a good beginner's sex toy, as they are not intimidating and are meant for ease of use.

procrasterbating
The act of masturbating as a form of procrastination. Very common in teenagers.

ProDom/ProDomme
A sex worker who specializes in BDSM, specifically in being a dominant partner for clients. Most of these dominants focus on domination techniques and punishment rather than actual penetrative or other kinds of focused sex. (A ProDom is male; a ProDomme is female).

professional submissive
A sex worker who specializes in BDSM, specifically in being a submissive partner for clients. The focus here is on receiving domination and not on any penetrative sex acts.

promiscuous
The word that describes someone who is characterized by a large number of sexual partners or by openness about their own sexuality. Often used in a derogatory way.

prostate
A muscular gland found in those with penises and testicles. This gland produces a white fluid that helps protect the sperm found in ejaculate. The prostate is extremely sensitive, and many anal sex acts focus on prostate stimulation in order to encourage intense orgasms. It is often referred to as the P-spot (see page 111).

prostate massage
The act of massaging, rubbing, or otherwise stimulating the prostate for sexual pleasure and intense orgasms. Also known as prostate milking.

prostate stimulator
A sex toy that is designed to stimulate a prostate. They are usually phallic, but with a curved or bulbous tip.

prostitute
An old, derogatory word for a sex worker.

protocol
The set of rules and behaviors agreed upon by all partners during the negotiation (see page 102) phase of a BDSM relationship. This includes the power exchange level (see page 134), any honorifics to be used (calling a dominant "Master" or "Daddy," for example), and any specific things that must be accomplished during a sexual encounter within the relationship.

PSE
An acronym for "porn star experience," a service offered by some sex workers that involves re-enacting scenes or taboo acts from a client's favorite pornographic film.

psychogenic erection
An erection that is caused by mental stimuli, rather than by direct, physical stimulation. Such erections are typically associated with fantasizing or with viewing erotic material.

psycholagny
The ability to have an orgasm without any physical stimulation, using only mental stimulation or the viewing of pornography or erotic media.

psychological bondage
A type of bondage that does not require any kind of physical restraint. Instead, a submissive is commanded not to move or to hold themselves in a specific way. Also referred to as "emotional bondage."

psychosexual
Related to the mental, emotional, or behavioral aspects of sexuality or sexual activity.

psychrophilia
Also known as psychrocism, this is a fetish for feeling extremely cold or freezing. Psychrophiliacs will often use ice in sexual practices, or will have sex in very cold rooms. They also enjoy watching others have sexual interactions in cold spaces or with frozen items.

pteronphilia
A fetish for the feeling of feathers on one's skin. A lot of adult stores sell peacock or other long feathers specifically for pteronphiles.

pubic hair
Hair that grows on or around the groin area. Pubic hair is often fetishized, and sexual cultures adopt specific types of care for pubic hair, such as cutting it into certain shapes.

pubic mound
The mass of fatty tissue found over the pubic bone in both males and females. Typically where pubic hair begins. In those with vaginas, the pubic mound forms the top of the vulva and labia majora.

public display of affection
Any semisexual or romantic act that takes place between partners in public (kissing, squeezing, waist holding, etc.). Often abbreviated as PDA.

public humiliation
A BDSM sex act that involves performing humiliation tactics on a submissive in public. Examples include being yelled at in public or being made to wear humiliating clothing.

pubococcygeus muscle
The hammock-shaped muscle found at the bottom of the

pelvic bone that supports all of the pelvic organs. Often abbreviated as the PC muscle.

pull-out method
A method of contraception for P-in-V (see page 124) sex that involves pulling the penis out of the vagina as soon as one starts to feel that ejaculation is imminent. The rate of effectiveness for the pull-out method is difficult to track, but most doctors agree that it is not the most effective contraceptive method.

pulsator
An electronic sex toy that utilizes pulsations to simulate the back-and-forth motions of penetrative sex.

pump gag
An inflatable gag that can be pumped up to a dominant's desired size. It can be very easy to overinflate a pump gag, which can cause suffocation. Most pump gags will have breathing tubes in them as a failsafe, but if yours doesn't, it's best to underinflate it to be on the safe side.

pump position
A penetrative sex position that uses a chair or sofa. The receiving partner straddles the chair, facing backwards, with their hands on the back of the chair. The giving partner sits on the chair behind them, facing the same direction. The receiving partner initiates penetration

by raising themself up slightly and then inserting when coming back down.

punishment tie
A type of bondage that is done for punishment. Punishment ties are expected to have a slight amount of pain associated with them to make the submissive uncomfortable.

puppy play
Any sex act that involves role-playing as a dog or using items associated with dogs, such as leashes or chew toys. People who engage in puppy play may lick their partners to show affection or bark instead of using words.

puppy-pile poly
1. A polyamorous relationship in which everyone involved is female.

2. A polyamorous relationship in which everyone involved is sexually/romantically active with one another.

pushing limits
In BDSM, the act of exploring and/or crossing agreed-upon soft boundaries. This is not necessarily a bad thing; during negotiation (see page 102), a submissive will note things that they haven't tried before, or have tried and not enjoyed, and a dominant may negotiate to try those things with the submissive at some point.

pushing rope
A slang term for trying to penetrate a partner with a semi-erect or flaccid penis.

pussy
A common slang term for a vagina.

pussy whipping
A type of BDSM play where the dominant partner will use their hand or a sex toy to hit their partner's vaginal area.

pussy worship
The practice of fetishizing and adoring vaginas, including giving cunnilingus (see page 46), massaging vaginas, engaging in vaginal intercourse, or otherwise interacting with vaginas. (Also see worship, page 225).

putting out
A slang term for engaging in sexual activity. It's often used to describe agreeing to sex quickly or without prompting.

PVC
A staple in the sex industry, PVC (which stands for poly-vinylchloride) is a type of plastic used to make sex toys, clothing, BDSM tools, and other staples of sexual play and enhancement. PVC is extremely inexpensive, making items molded with it very affordable for consumers. However, PVC does contain higher amounts of chemicals

than most other materials and has gained criticism for its continued use.

pygophilia
A fetish for buttocks, including looking at butts or feeling butts.

pyrolagnia
A fetish for very large fires or for creatures or people associated with fire, such as dragons or firefighters.

pyrophilia
A fetish for fire or items related to fire, such as candles, lighters, stovetops, matches, or campfires.

Q

quad

A polyamorous relationship involving exactly four people. Each person does not necessarily engage with all the others, and may only be tied to one other member of the group.

queef

A noise that occurs when air is trapped in a vagina and then rushes out. This is very common during penetrative intercourse, where the penetrating item pushes air into the vaginal canal and then allows it to escape.

queening stool

A low stool or seat shaped like a U, with ample open space in the middle. The stool is placed over a person's face, and a person with a vagina will sit on top of the stool, giving them a comfortable seat while their partner performs cunnilingus (see page 46).

queer

1. A term for people who do not identify as heterosexual, or as strictly male or female.

2. A general term for anyone whose sexuality or gender falls outside the "norm." *Queer* is seen as a more inclusive term than *LGBT* (page 93), as it doesn't single out any specific sexualities or genders.

queer bait

A heterosexual person who may be mistaken for someone with a queer sexuality.

questioning

The term for someone who is unsure of their sexuality, sexual preferences, or gender. Questioning does not necessarily end when a person takes on a sexual identity; it may continue for one's entire life. Questioning is meant to be a period of reflection about what one does and does not like, either about oneself or how one experiences sex.

quickie

A quick, possibly spontaneous sexual encounter.

R

rabbit vibrator

A type of phallic sex toy with an extension, traditionally shaped like a pair of rabbit ears, that is meant for stimulating a clitoris.

race play

BDSM and role-playing scenarios in which the partners involved act out historical or other events in which race is an important or distinguishing factor

RACK

An acronym for risk-aware consensual kink; a BDSM practice that encourages all participants in a sexual activity to understand the risks of that activity. For example, whipping someone may lead to bruises; a submissive who practices RACK will understand and accept that.

ravishment fantasy
A sexual fantasy involving a person who cannot resist their partner and would do anything to have sex with them (excluding sexual assault). Most of these fantasies are sensual rather than forceful.

raw jaw
A slang term for oral sex on a penis that is not covered with a condom.

reach around
A type of hand job (see page 74) where the giving partner stands behind the receiving partner and reaches around the receiving partner's waist in order to masturbate their genitals.

rear entry
Any penetrative sex act where the penetration takes place from behind the receiving partner.

reclining lotus position
A penetrative sex position; this is the reverse of the lotus blossom position (see page 94) and puts the giving partner on top. The receiving partner sits with legs crossed (lotus style, if possible, where each ankle is on the opposite knee). The giving partner then kneels in front of the receiving partner and initiates penetration.

redhead fetish
A fetish or sexual preference for partners who have red hair.

refractory period
The period of time between orgasm and the time when the penis is able to become erect again. The length of the refractory period is different for each individual, and some people may be able to maintain an erection very shortly after orgasm.

relationship orientation
The type of relationship that a person chooses to have, whether monogamous, polyamorous, open, or otherwise.

relationship structure
The agreed-upon set of rules in a romantic or sexual relationship of any kind.

religious play
Role-playing involving religious characters (such as a priest or a rabbi) or situations, or the use of religious objects (such as sacramental candles) in sexual activities. There are also organized sex groups that are dedicated to religious play; groups like this are part of the religious scene. (Also see hierophilia, page 78).

remote-control sex toy
An electronic sex toy that can be operated wirelessly and remotely. This is great for BDSM-practicing or kinky couples who want to give each other pleasure while out in public or while in different rooms.

requirement limit
The list of things that must happen in a BDSM activity for the dominant or submissive to achieve sexual satisfaction. For example, a dominant might require oral sex during every activity, or a submissive might require being spanked. These requirements will be figured out in the negotiation phase (see negotiation, page 102).

resistance play
Any type of sexual activity where one or more partner pretends to resist sexual advances.

retrograde ejaculation
A sexual condition in which the semen produced by the testicles is released into the bladder during ejaculation instead of going out through the urethra. This is what causes a "dry" orgasm. This typically means the bladder sphincter is not functioning correctly.

reverse cowgirl position
A penetrative sex position in which the giving partner lies on their back, and the receiving partner straddles the giving

partner, but facing the opposite direction (so the receiving partner should be facing the giving partner's feet).

reverse prayer bondage
A BDSM binding position in which a submissive's arms are tied behind their back in a way that makes it so their hands are touching, palm to palm.

rhabdophilia
A fetish for being flogged or beaten. Rhabdophiliacs need to feel a beating themselves; they are not typically aroused by watching others being beaten.

riding astride position
A penetrative sex position that is also a leg workout for the receiving partner! The giving partner lies down on a flat, sturdy surface, together. The receiving partner straddles the giving partner with feet flat on the floor, in a squatting position, and initiates penetration.

riding crop
One of the most popular BDSM toys, this is a short, rigid whip that usually has a flexible loop or paddle on the end of it. Being hit with a riding crop will sting slightly, but will not cause great harm to a submissive.

rigger
A person who celebrates the art of bondage. Riggers are

often called upon by BDSM couples to bind a submissive, though the rigger may not participate in any sexual activities. Many riggers will bind consenting models and take pictures or video for pornographic sale or artistic use.

rimming/rim job
A slang term for analingus (see page 19).

ring gag
A BDSM sex toy that is used to hold a submissive's mouth open. This type of gag utilizes a large metal ring with straps tied to either side of it. The ring is inserted into the mouth, typically inside the lips, and the straps are tied behind the head to hold it in place.

ring of O
A special type of ring worn by a BDSM practitioner to signal their interest in BDSM to others. Also known as a Roissy ring.

In today's world, wearing jewelry or clothes with symbols that pay homage to a TV show, movie, or book is very common. It makes sense that when the BDSM community was looking for a way to outwardly signify their sexuality, they turned to one of the most famous stories about BDSM, *The Story of O*. The novel, written by Pauline Réage and published in France in 1954 (the English version was published in 1965), is about a woman who is taught to be a fully submissive sexual partner by a series of dominating men. This book caused a ton of controversy when it was first released to the public, inciting bans of the book in areas throughout the country; conservative people hated the book for the flagrant sexual acts portrayed, and feminists hated it because they believe the book championed the abuse of women. But those in the BDSM community quickly flocked to the story, and it has been a staple for those interested in the extremes of BDSM ever since.

---

ripped clothes fetish

A fetish for ripping clothes off an individual before sexual activity, or for having one's own clothes ripped off.

road head

Oral sex performed on a receiving partner who is driving.

robot fetish

An intense sexual attraction to robots or androids, including any electronic machinery that adheres to the laws of robotics, or anything that presents as a robot (such as a person in a robot costume). Individuals with a robot fetish will often refer to themselves as technosexuals (see page 202).

rocker

A chairlike sex toy that simulates the thrusting of penetrative intercourse. A rocker consists of two connected padded stools with a bit of space in the middle; this space holds a dildo or other penetrative toy that is connected to a lever. The user will sit on the rocker and insert the dildo into themself. They can then either use their hand to move the lever, or rock back and forth to mimic the thrusting motion of penetrative sex.

rod
1. A slang term for a penis.

2. In BDSM, a thin cane used to strike someone.

rod rash
The slang term for penis chafing caused by excessive sexual activity.

role reversal
In terms of sexuality, this refers to any act where a partner performs the opposite of their typical sexual role. This could be something like a submissive taking on a dominant role, or a person who is usually a receiving partner during sex acting as a giving partner.

role-playing
The act of temporarily assuming the role of a different person, object, or animal. For sexual purposes, this means dressing up as or pretending to be a fetishized thing during sexual activities, and often during play (see page 125) experiences. For example, people who love pirate play might dress up as pirates during sex and talk in pirate speak.

roman shower
A sex act in which those with emetophilia (see page 56) vomit on each other for sexual enjoyment.

rope bondage
Any BDSM, kink, or sex act that uses rope to restrict or bind a participant. There are many styles of rope bondage, including partial rope bondage (binding of one part of the body), Western-style rope bondage, shibari (which originated in Japan and tends to be more sensual and ritualistic), and suspension bondage (in which rope is used to suspend someone from an elevated object).

rope bunny
In BDSM, a slang term for someone who loves to be put into very tight or inescapable rope bondage.

rope cuff
A knot that binds a submissive's wrists or ankles.

rope dress
The term for rope bondage which wraps around the entire body. Typically made of intricate knots, a rope dress will not necessarily cover every inch of skin, but will always be placed on strategic parts of the body, such as the breasts or pelvic area, to apply pressure to those areas.

rope gag
A sexual gag made of a knotted rope ball with a rope string on each end.

RTF
An acronym for "return to fuck"; a rating term for sex workers, commonly used in online forums to denote a good sexual experience with a particular person. If a rating says "RTF," it means that the reviewer intends to patronize that sex worker again in the future, and recommends them as a sexual companion.

rubber
A slang term for a condom.

rubber ducky vibrator
A small, powerful vibrating sex toy that is shaped like the popular children's bath toy, the rubber duck. A lot of people like this toy because it can be left around the house and will not be questioned by someone who finds it.

ruined orgasms
A sexual practice that involves one partner vigorously stimulating the other until they are about to orgasm and then suddenly stopping the stimulation. This is different from edging (see page 56), where sexual activities will pause to stave off orgasm for a length of time. For a ruined orgasm, all sexual activity will cease, typically causing the person

on the receiving end to feel frustrated and sometimes in pain. If the encounter stops and orgasm happens anyway, the orgasm tends to be less intense than normal.

rump raid
A slang term for any sex act in which something is inserted into the anus.

rusty trombone
A sex act which combines analingus (see page 19) with a reach around (see page 150).

S

sadism
The act of experiencing pleasure when inflicting pain on others.

sadomasochism
The combination of sadism and masochism, either in a sexual act or within one person's sexual preferences. Sadomasochists love both inflicting pain on others and having pain inflicted upon them.

safer sex
Any sexual activity where all partners use precautions against STIs and pregnancy.

safe, sane, consensual
A BDSM philosophy that states that sexual activities should minimize risks, be approached with a clear frame of mind, and be consented to by all participants.

safe-sex circle
A relationship structure (see page 151) in which all partners agree to have barrier-free sexual contact only with the other partners in the circle. If sexual activities are allowed outside of the group, then they must always use preventive measures, such as condoms. This is also known as a "condom contract."

safeword
A code word that is used by submissives during BDSM activities to signal that an activity has reached the edge of their limits, or that something has gone wrong and they need to stop. Safewords are always agreed upon beforehand, and the dominant partner must cease their activity upon hearing the safeword. Safewords are also not limited to verbal cues; if both partners agree to it, they may be another sound or physical act, such as whistling or snapping.

salirophilia
A fetish for soiling or defacing a specific person or object of the salirophiliac's desire. This could mean making an object dirty, breaking an object, or defiling a person in some way.

sapiosexuality
A type of sexuality in which sexual attraction to others is based solely on intelligence, rather than physicality. Sapiosexuals are not blind to the physical body—it's just not

where their sexual attraction is centered. Some sapiosexuals refer to themselves as "nymphobrainiacs."

sapphic
An adjective for any sex act involving two women. The word is an homage to the Greek poet Sappho, who was believed to be a lesbian.

satin fetish
A fetish for satin—wearing it, seeing someone else wear it, or feeling it on one's body. Satin fetishes are common in the crossdressing community, because many forms of women's lingerie are made of satin; both silk and satin are regarded as very feminine fabrics.

sausage party
A slang term for an orgy or other sexual event where the participants are mostly (or solely) male.

scarf position
A rear-entry penetrative sex position in which the receiving partner lies facedown and lifts up their legs behind them. The giving partner will kneel behind the receiving partner's crotch and put the receiving partner's legs on the giving partner's shoulders. They can then penetrate the receiving partner deeply. This position also works very well for cunnilingus.

scarfing
A type of erotic asphyxiation (see asphyxiophilia, page 23) that involves tying a scarf around the neck to limit oxygen.

scat play
Any sexual activity that involves feces. (Also see coprophilia, page 43).

scene
The term for any BDSM encounter between two or more partners. Penetrative sex isn't necessarily involved, but participants may use BDSM toys or participate in BDSM acts in a scene.

scent play/smell play
A kink/BDSM act where submissives or partners will be forced or asked to smell areas of the dominant's or another partner's body, clothing, or other personal items.

schoolgirl fetish
A fetish for things that are associated with schoolgirls, particularly ones in private schools with uniforms and strict rules. Those with a schoolgirl fetish enjoy seeing their partner dressed in a school uniform, and they may enjoy role-playing as a young person in school, with tests and young love to deal with.

scissor position
A sex position meant for two partners with vaginas. Each partner lies on their side, but overlapping, and with the heads in opposite directions (so that the knees are aligned). Each partner opens their legs slightly and then intertwines them so that their groins are touching. They can then stimulate their clitorises and vaginas by rubbing against each other.

scissor sister
A slang term for a lesbian.

scold's bridle
A metal muzzle and head cage combination that is used in BDSM play. The cage, which can be locked from the outside, is slipped over the head. The muzzle, which may have a bit inside of it designed to go into a submissive's mouth, is put over the mouth area to restrict speech.

screwing
A slang term for penetrative sex.

scrotal inflation/scrotal infusion
The act of injecting liquid into the scrotum in order to make the scrotal sac appear larger. The liquid is then absorbed into the body over several days. This process can also be done with air or gas, though it is not as common.

*Note: extended practice of scrotal inflation can cause definite harm, such as infection or infertility. Please take this into account if you choose to practice and if you feel any intense pain in your scrotum, contact emergency services or your doctor immediately.

scrotum

Also known as the scrotal sac, this is the pouch of skin and muscle located underneath the penis. The scrotum protects the testicles from harm, and also helps to keep the testicles at the optimal temperature.

seated scissor position

A penetrative sex position that is a variation of the reverse cowgirl position (see page 152). The receiving partner positions their feet so one foot is between the giving partner's legs and the other is outside. This turns the receiving partner slightly to the side for a different kind of penetrative experience.

secondary

A person in a polyamorous (see polyamory, page 128) or other multi-person relationship who is less significant to the relationship than a primary (see page 137). Secondaries may be casual lovers or long-term boyfriends/girlfriends/paramours (see page 115) who are given less time, energy, and priority than a primary.

secretary fetish
A fetish for secretaries or for using objects or items that are associated with secretaries in sexual acts.

seduction
The act of attempting to engage a partner in sexual activities by sparking sexual desires in that person.

seduction position
A penetrative or cunnilingus/analingus sex position in which the receiving partner sits on their knees, then bends forward so that their head is almost on the floor. The giving partner can then proceed with oral sex or penetration.

see-saw position
A penetrative sex position that is a variation on the cowgirl position. Both partners have their legs outstretched and slightly elevated, and the receiving partner will lean back on their hands. This gives the appearance of a see-saw and allows the receiving partner to rock or grind on the giving partner's groin.

self bondage
A BDSM masturbatory act in which someone will bind themself in some way before masturbation. This is typically done with handcuffs or simple knots, as the binding needs to be easy to undo alone.

*Note: before attempting self bondage, it is recommended that you read tutorials on how to do it properly. You should be able to remove your bindings by yourself, so if there is an emergency, such as a fire, you will be able to escape.

self love
A slang term for masturbation.

self service
A slang term for masturbation.

semen
The white or gray liquid that is ejaculated from the penis during an orgasm. Semen consists mostly of a fluid that is secreted from the prostate gland, mixed with sperm (see page 190).

sennet whip
A BDSM sex toy consisting of an eighteen- to twenty-four-inch pleated cord and knot covered in stiff tar or wax, which is meant to increase the weight and impact of the whip.

sensate focus
An erotic act and series of exercises that has couples focus on the senses they use during sexual acts. Touch is a major component of the exercises, and partners are taught to touch each other in a very aware manner. These kinds of exercises can increase both romantic and sexual attraction between partners.

sensation play
Any sex act that places emphasis on heightened senses; for example, using aroma during a sex act, or rubbing skin with an ice cube.

sensory deprivation play
A kink or BDSM sex act in which one or more of a submissive's or partner's senses are deprived. This could include blindfolding a partner to deprive them of sight or covering their ears to prohibit hearing.

sensual bondage
Bondage that is tied in such a way that it gives pleasure to the bound person, rather than being purely for restriction.

sensual domination
A type of domination where the acts performed are all designed to be extremely pleasurable for the submissive person; for example, binding a submissive and then performing oral sex on them.

sensualist
Someone who is obsessed with giving and receiving strictly pleasure. Sensualists do not engage in pain for pleasure.

serial monogamy
A relationship pattern in which someone has only long, monogamous relationships and does not engage in casual sex.

serpent's tongue
A BDSM whip with a V-shaped topper, typically made of leather or suede. Also known as a serpent's kiss. Gentle use of this toy can simulate the feeling of a snake's tongue on the body.

service gag
A type of gag that has room for an attachment in front of it, so that the submissive person can perform tasks (sexual or otherwise) for their dominant partner. Attachments include dildos, brushes, feathers, and other instruments of sex.

service top
A submissive who will also perform dominant activities if asked by their dominant partner.

session
Any period of sexual activity that is paid for, particularly with a ProDom or ProDomme (see page 139).

Sex 4.0
A term used by some to refer to the modern-day sexual revolution. Ideas about sex and the way we culturally view and treat sex are continually changing, and with the addition of increasingly rapid technological advancements in the sex world, current changes are seen as more extreme than those that took place at any other point in history.

sex addiction
A sexual condition in which someone feels constant compulsive urges to have sex or participate in sexual activity.

sex chair
A piece of furniture that is designed to support bodies in positions that might not be possible with regular furniture. These chairs help elevate the body for different kinds of stimulation, and can provide deeper penetrative experiences.

sex coach
A hirable professional trained to help clients with any sexual disorders, misgivings, or achievements that they would like to accomplish. If someone has had trouble experiencing an orgasm, for example, they might hire a sex coach to teach them new and better climaxing techniques for their own body.

sex cushion/sex pillow
A cushion or pillow designed to be used on or underneath a body during sex. They come in several different styles, including flat types for elevation or curved ones to help initiate a rocking motion.

sex education
Educational classes or materials that teach people (though

typically children and teenagers ages eight to eighteen) about human sexuality and reproduction. In many countries, sex education takes place in schools, but since each area and school administration has differing views on sex, the class content varies wildly.

sex educator
A person who is certified to teach people about sex and sexuality. There are many ways to become certified: the most common way is through the American Association of Sex Educators, Counselors, and Therapists (AASECT), but there are also many colleges offering master's programs in sex therapy (see page 172) and sexology (see page 174).

sex game
Any game that involves sex or takes place during a sexual activity. Examples include strip poker and naked Twister.

sex geek
A term for individuals who are obsessed with the nuances of sex. These people take great pride in learning all there is to know about sex, including positions, sexualities, media, and more.

sex hangups
Anxieties that come about by thinking about a certain type of sexuality, sexual act, or sexual object.

sex machine
An electronic sex toy that simulates intercourse or oral sex. Sex machines typically utilize motors attached to a long metal rod with a dildo on the end; the dildo can be thrusted in and out of any orifice. Attachments are often interchangeable; some can utilize suction or simulate oral sex. The machines can be adjusted for speed and intensity.

sex ramp
A piece of sex furniture shaped like a wedge which is meant to lift different parts of the body during sex.

sex shop
Also known as an adult shop, this is a type of shop that sells products meant to enhance sexual experiences, such as sex toys, lubricants, lingerie, and pornography.

sex swing
A type of sex furniture, also known as a sex sling, which restrains a person so that they are suspended in the air. Sex swings are usually made of leather or fabric straps, which can be fastened around the waist, ankles, legs, arms, and wrists, and have chains that can be attached to the ceiling or walls at any height.

sex therapist
A psychiatrist that is trained specifically to help people with their sexual relationships and feelings. Unlike sex

coaches (see page 170), sex therapists will not give physical aid; they focus on treating sexual disorders and hangups, as well as helping couples work through any issues that may be hindering their sex life.

sex worker
A term used to describe anyone who works in the sex industry, particularly those who directly exchange money for sex, but also phone-sex agents, escorts, or those who work in pornography.

sexcellence
A sexual philosophy that promotes experimentation with and study of many different sexualities, sex positions, and kinks with the goal of becoming an excellent partner in any sexual situation. Sexcellence is a portmanteau of "sex" and "excellence."

sexercise
Any physical exercise that is performed in order to tone and build the muscles used for sexual activities. The goal of any sexercise regimen is to hone one's body into a sex machine, to have the stamina and build to perform any kind of sex position, and to improve the flow of oxygenated blood to the genitalia.

sexercism
A slang term for having casual sex or a one-night stand in

order to forget about a previous sexual or romantic relationship. A portmanteau of "sex" and "exorcism."

sex-negative
An adjective that describes a person or attitude that is critical of or very uncomfortable with sex or sexuality.

sexology
The academic and scientific study of sex and sexuality, including how sexuality develops, the history of human sexual behavior, the creation of new STIs and finding cures/treatments, and the study of sexual conditions.

sex-positive
An adjective that describes a person or attitude that embraces sex and promotes healthy sexuality. Sex-positive people encourage any and all consensual sexual acts.

sexsomnia
Also known as "sleep sex," this is a sexual condition that causes sufferers to initiate sexual behaviors (usually without realizing they are doing so) during non-REM sleep.

sextasy
The term for ingesting Viagra (see page 218) and the illegal drug Ecstasy, with the goal of having more intense sexual intercourse that lasts for a very long time.

sexting
The act of texting someone erotic or sexually explicit messages via cell phone or computer messaging program. It is similar to phone sex (see page 121), except using the written word instead of talking.

sexual aversion disorder
A sexual condition that causes one to feel distressed about and recoil from any sexual contact or the thought of sex. While this does occur on its own, it could also be caused by trauma from sexual abuse (see page 237).

sexual compatibility
The term for the affinity between partners who have matching sexual desires, leading to the possibility of increased sexual satisfaction.

Sexual Compulsives Anonymous
An organized group, abbreviated as SCA, designed to help those with hypersexuality (see page 81) control their sexual instincts. SCA utilizes a twelve-step program to help participants understand what is happening in their brains and teach them how to express their sexuality in a healthy way.

sexual discomfort
Any undesired pain that comes from a sexual activity.

sexual health

The physical, emotional, and mental state of sexual well-being. To be sexually healthy means to be respectful of one's own desires and the desires of others, to practice safe sex or understand the risks of unsafe sex, and to have sex only with consenting individuals.

sexual imprinting

The process that mammals, including humans, use to determine the best qualities and characteristics of potential mates or sexual partners. While animals will use predetermined criteria such as scents, fur, plumage, and feats of strength to determine who will be a good mate, humans each develop their own personal judgement style, which may be based on things learned in childhood, preferred physical features, skills, and many other things.

sexual performance anxiety

A sexual condition that causes a person to constantly worry about their sexual performance and whether their partners are experiencing sexual satisfaction. This disorder can affect anyone, though it seems to be much more prevalent in those with penises.

sexual pleasure

The term for the physical and mental pleasure that is directly caused by sexual stimulation.

sexual repression

A state of being in which someone cannot express their sexuality. Such repression can be caused by a mental or social issue.

sexual response

The response of the physical body when presented with sexual opportunity or stimulation.

Sexual response is a four-part process. The first phase is known as excitement or arousal. The body starts to heat up, and the sexual organs are filled with blood, signaling readiness for sexual contact. This is the phase during which partners can engage in foreplay and explore each other's bodies in a state that feels good for an extended time. The second is the plateau phase, the state between excitement and climax, where the body may become tense and the heart rate increases to prepare for phase three—orgasm. Orgasm is the release of sexual tension, either through ejaculation or muscle contractions (or both). The last phase is resolution, where the body relaxes and all sexual organs return to their pre-excitement state.

SGL

An acronym for "same gender loving"; a term used primarily by the African American community to refer to those who identify as gay or lesbian.

shackles
Metal restraints that are placed around the ankles to limit the movement of a submissive. Shackles look like two thick metal rings, typically connected by a weighted chain.

shaft
The length of the penis between the scrotum and the penis head. The shaft is comprised of three cylinders of soft tissue which are filled with lots of blood vessels. During arousal, these vessels fill with blood to create an erection.

shaggable
A slang term for someone who is sexually attractive. Although the term has been around for a while, it was popularized by the movie *Austin Powers*.

shinju
A type of rope bondage harness designed to fit over and restrain female breasts.

shocker
A type of hand job performed on those with vaginas, where the giving partner will insert two or three fingers into the vaginal canal and one or two fingers into the anus to masturbate both at the same time.

shoe fetish
A fetish for shoes. This includes all types of footwear,

though most fetishists will focus on extreme shoes, such as very high heels, shoes made of odd materials or with odd shapes, or shoes with embellishments like spikes or rhinestones.

shooting blanks
A slang term for male ejaculation where the semen contains a diminished amount of sperm, making conception much more difficult to achieve.

shower sex
A term for any sexual activity that takes place in a shower.

shrimp tie
A rope bondage (see page 157) position where a submissive's hands are bound to the opposite elbows. The chest is restrained, possibly with a shinju (see page 178), and the legs are tied together, creating the appearance of a shrimp.

shrimping
The erotic act of sucking the toes of a sexual partner.

side to side
A sex position that is a variation on the missionary position. Both partners lie on their sides facing each other and entwine their legs. Penetration or sexual rubbing can then be initiated.

siderodromophilia
A fetish for trains and anything related to trains, including being on a train, seeing a train, standing on train tracks, or wearing old conductors' uniforms.

signal whip
A very long (three to four feet), braided whip used for BDSM practices. The braiding prevents fraying, and the length allows it to wrap around a body. Signal whips were originally designed to be used on sled dogs during races.

significant other
A term that typically indicates a boyfriend, girlfriend, or spouse, though it is a general term and can be applied to any romantic or sexual situation in which there is a close, intimate relationship.

silicone lubricant
A lubricant made primarily out of silicone, designed to be used for vaginal and anal penetration. Silicone lubricant will not be absorbed into the skin, making it a good choice for prolonged sexual sessions.

single glove
A BDSM sex toy that binds the hands and wrists together.

sitophilia
A fetish for food, including eating food, watching a

partner eat, and sights, smells, or sounds associated with food. Sitophiles may also experience arousal from cooking or visiting restaurants.

sitting position
A penetrative sex position in which the giving partner sits on a bed or other surface with legs spread. The receiving partner will then lie in front of the giving partner and put their legs on the giving partner's shoulders, allowing easy access to orifices.

sjambok
A heavy BDSM whip traditionally made from animal hide, but more commonly made of plastic today.

Skene's glands
The glands on either side of the vagina, close to the urethra. Since the ducts from these glands empty into the urethra, it is speculated that they are the source of vaginal ejaculate.

skirt fetish
A sexual fascination with skirts, including wearing skirts or seeing a partner in a skirt.

skoliosexual
A person who is attracted strictly to those who identify outside of the male/female gender binary. A skoliosexual

might pursue a relationship with an intersex or nonbinary person.

skull fuck
A slang term for any intense oral sex session, though it typically refers to fellatio where a receiving partner will vigorously thrust themselves into their partner's mouth.

slapper
A type of paddle (see page 112) with a second layer of leather attached, which makes a slapping sound on impact.

slave
A name for a submissive partner in a Master/slave relationship, a type of BDSM relationship that involves strict control. The Master/slave relationship goes even further than a typical dominant/submissive relationship. Slaves are always under their Master's or Mistress's control in sexual, social, and domestic situations; they are essentially used as property. This type of relationship is always negotiated and consensual.

slave auction
A BDSM event at which self-designated slaves are auctioned off to dominant Masters and Mistresses, either for a night or for an extended relationship.

sleep masturbation
A common sexual condition in which people masturbate while sleeping. This often comes as a result of having a sexual dream. Sleep masturbation is not typically considered a cause for alarm.

slippery nipple position
An easy penetrative sex position in which the receiving partner will lie flat on a bed or other raised piece of furniture, close to the edge. The giving partner will sit on the edge of the bed, straddling the receiving partner, with one leg up on the bed and the other leg on the floor. The giving partner will do the bulk of the penetrative work here; this position is known to be very good for burning extra calories for the giving partner.

slow dance position
The missionary position of standing penetrative sex positions. Partners face each other while standing and initiate penetration, using a stepstool to adjust for height if necessary.

slut
1. A sexually promiscuous person; someone who loves sexual relationships and pursues many of them.

2. A derogatory term used against someone, particularly a woman, who expresses sexual desires.

3. A term for someone who fetishizes or is obsessed with something. For example, someone with a foot fetish might call themselves a "foot slut."

slut shaming
Enforcing the social stigma against those considered "sluts" or those who act outside of typical sexual behavior for their time or culture.

slut training
A BDSM regimen where submissives are taught by their dominants how to behave in a slutty manner that pleases the dominant. Not all slut training is the same, though they all encourage submissives to act outside of cultural norms in public.

smexy
A portmanteau of "smart" and "sexy"; a slang adjective for someone who is attractive both physically and intellectually.

smoking fetish
A fetish for smoking or for watching others smoke cigarettes, cigars, pipes, or hookahs. Even the smell of smoke may arouse someone with a smoking fetish.

smotherbox
A fetish item similar to a body bag that is made to cover

a person's entire body except for their mouth; the mouth opening is there to facilitate the giving of oral sex. (Also see mummification, page 100).

smothering
A type of erotic asphyxiation (see asphyxiophilia, page 23), smothering is the term for blocking off a partner's airways for pleasure during a sexual activity by placing an item, such as a hand or a pillow, over the mouth or nostrils.

* Note: extended coverage of the mouth or nostrils can cause asphyxiation, which can lead to fainting or even death. If you choose to engage in smothering, it is recommended that you only do so for short period of time per each smothering act.

smudged makeup fetish
A fetish for seeing a partner with smudged, ruined, or running makeup during sexual activity.

snake charmer
A challenging fellatio position in which the receiving partner goes into a handstand, with or without an object for support. The giving partner is then able to perform fellatio while standing up.

snatch
A slang term for *vagina*. Some consider this an offensive term that is used to degrade women.

sneezing fetish
A fetish for sneezing, watching or hearing others sneeze, or thinking about sneezing.

snowballing
A sex act in which a partner with a penis will ejaculate into another partner's mouth. The second partner will then pass the ejaculate back to the first partner or on to a third partner by kissing them. Also known as snowblowing.

social model of sexuality
A sexual philosophy that states sex and sexuality are not things that are simply experienced and shaped through the body, but are shaped by cultural, familial, and psychological influences. The model is quickly becoming a focus of study for sexologists (see page 174).

sock fetish
A sexual fascination with socks, including wearing socks, seeing a partner in a specific type of sock (knee socks, ankle socks, fuzzy socks, etc.), or buying socks.

sodomy
A general term for any kind of sex that does not lead to reproduction. This includes oral sex, anal sex, and masturbation.

soft swap
A swinging (see page 198) term for swapping spouses for a set amount of time for any sex acts except penetration.

soft swinger
A partner in a swinging relationship who only participates in soft swaps.

softcore
Any pornographic media that shows nude or semi-nude people who are not engaging in sex acts. Softcore porn is meant to be erotic or sensual.

solicitation
The act of offering money or goods in exchange for sexual favors, either from a sex worker or otherwise. Solicitation is illegal in most parts of the world.

solo poly
A type of polyamory (see page 198) where one person seeks out multiple sexual relationships but will not engage in traditional romantic partnerships with any of their sex partners, instead choosing to focus emotional energy on the self.

solosexual
Someone who prefers masturbation to partnered sex. Solosexuals may choose to have romantic relationships

with another person, but they generally choose to be by themselves.

SOMF
An acronym for "sit on my face"; slang for facesitting (see page 61).

sororal polygyny
A polygamous marriage in which a man is married to two or more women who are related to each other, typically sisters. Also known as sororate marriage.

south of the border
A slang term for the groin area.

southern exposure position
An oral sex position in which the receiving partner lies on their back, lifts their knees to their chest, and spreads their legs as wide as they wish. The giving partner can then perform oral sex by placing their head between the receiving partner's lifted legs.

spandex fetish
A fetish for clothing or other items made of spandex, a stretchy, rubbery fabric which is often referred to as a "second skin." Spandex is often used in lingerie items and sex toys.

spank the monkey
A slang term for masturbating a penis.

spanking
The practice of slapping a partner, on the bottom or elsewhere, for sexual pleasure, using one's bare hand or a sex toy.

spanking bench
A small bench covered in padding which a person can be bent over without discomfort, making spanking them much easier.

spanking glove
A glove, typically made of rubber or spandex, that is worn by someone who is spanking a partner. The glove is meant to protect the spanker's hand from impact irritation.

spanking skirt
A skirt that is designed to be opened easily from the back so that the wearer can be spanked.

spectatoring
The act of focusing on one's own performance during sexual activities instead of being in the moment or enjoying the sensations of sex, making one more of a spectator than a participant.

spectraromantic
One who is attracted romantically to a wide variety of genders or sexualities.

spectrasexual
One who is attracted sexually to a wide variety of genders or sexualities.

spectrophilia
A fetish for ghosts or imagined ghostly encounters. Those with spectrophilia do not necessarily need a visual component to their fetish, but may become aroused simply by the thought of ghosts or of a ghost being near.

sperm
The reproductive sex cells that are produced by those with testicles. Sperm makes up about 2 to 5 percent of semen by volume.

People with testes actually have a maximum capacity for sperm storage; sperm is created at such a high rate that often the release of sperm from the body in semen cannot keep up with all of the sperm being produced, especially if the person in question has not had sexual release for a long time. Luckily, the human body evolved to be able to recycle old sperm into the body; sperm that have been inside the seminal vesicles (essentially sperm holding areas) for too long are broken down and reabsorbed by the body for other uses.

spermicide
A substance that immobilizes and kills sperm. Spermicide can be rubbed on the inside of any orifice as a contraceptive before penetrative sex.

sphincter
The opening to the anal canal which consists of two parts, the ani externus and the ani internus, the first being the external opening of the anus, and the second the internal opening that surrounds a small area of the upper anal canal. This also includes the sphincter muscles. For anal sex to occur, the receiving partner needs to relax the entirety of their sphincter in order to allow penetration.

spinner
A term used in the pornography industry for a small, petite woman who has a lot of physical agility that can be used for sexual activity.

spit fuck
A slang term for any sexual activity where spit is used as a lubricant.

splitting bamboo position
A penetrative sex position made famous by the Kama Sutra (see page 88), where the receiving partner lies on their back with one leg extended into the air. The giving partner can then hold on to that leg for deeper penetration.

sploosh
A slang exclamation indicating sexual arousal. Popularized by the TV show *Archer*.

spooning
Romantic cuddling where two or more partners lie on their sides facing the same direction, so that one partner's front is touching the other's back. The person whose back is being touched is called the "little spoon," and the other person is the "big spoon."

spooning position
A penetrative sex position identical to spooning (see previous definition), with the giving partner acting as the big spoon. Also referred to as "sporking," a combination of "spooning" and "forking."

spread-eagle position
A cunnilingus position where the receiver lies on their back with all of their limbs outstretched, allowing the giving partner much more control over the receiving partner. The limbs might also be restrained with rope or other bondage material.

spreader bar
A metal bar that is used to keep a submissive's limbs apart during bondage. Some spreader bars have cuffs or other restraints built into them.

spunk
A slang term for semen.

squeeze technique
An edging (see page 56) technique in which a partner with a penis will squeeze their penis as soon as they feel orgasm coming on. This can delay the orgasm for a little while, but will generally need to be repeated for prolonged delay.

squick
The feeling of repulsion some people get when hearing or reading about kinky sexual acts.

squirter
A person with a vagina who experiences vaginal ejaculation. (It is not currently known whether all people with vaginas can be squirters, but only a small percentage of people with vaginas report having experienced squirting).

St. Andrew's cross
A type of BDSM furniture used for restraining a submissive's body in a standing spread-eagle position. The St. Andrew's cross is made of two pieces of wood or other firm material that are joined into an X shape and mounted on a balanced stand. This is also referred to as an X-frame.

standing 69 position
An oral sex position where one partner will stand upright and the other will get into a handstand position in front of them, and facing them, so that each person's head is between the other's thighs. Both partners can then initiate oral sex.

starfish
The term for a person who is typically a receiving partner during sex who does not actively participate. A starfish will simply lie on a surface and allow the sex to happen to them.

STI
An acronym for "sexually transmitted infection"; these types of diseases can be contracted through physical sexual activities. STIs typically affect the sexual organs, including causing painful inflammation, bumps, or rashes on the penis or vagina, but there are some that can affect the entire body. They are sometimes known as STDs (for "sexually transmitted diseases"). Practicing safe sex greatly reduces the risk of catching an STI.

steel bondage
Any BDSM bondage that uses metal materials for binding, including handcuffs or chains.

stiffy
A slang term for an erection.

stigmatophilia
A sexual fascination with partners who have been physically scarred, tattooed, or pierced.

stone butches
A lesbian who chooses to present in a more masculine way. Stone butches usually do not like to be touched in their genital region, but prefer to focus on sexually satisfying their partner.

strap-on
A phallic object, such as a dildo or vibrator, which is placed into a harness and worn over the stomach or crotch. By wearing the strap-on, the person can then penetrate their partner as someone with a penis would.

strappado bondage
A type of sexual bondage where a submissive's arms are tied together behind their back and then lifted into the air further and further, until the submissive needs to lean forward in order to keep the position.

streetwalker
A sex worker who looks for clients by walking the streets and inquiring subtly through body language and coded speak.

stretcher
A type of sex toy that is designed to stretch a specific part of the body, but typically the genitals. There are scrotum stretchers, anus stretchers, vaginal stretchers, labia stretchers, and more.

stud
A slang term for someone, typically a man, who is extremely physically attractive and who has sex with many different, typically female partners.

stunt cock
Just as a stunt person in the film industry performs action stunts that the celebrity actors cannot do, a stunt cock takes the place of a porn actor for close-ups or ejaculation shots.

stygiophilia
A fetish for the thought of a torturous afterlife, including hell, hellfire, eternal torture, and damnation.

sub frenzy
The term for when a submissive in a BDSM relationship has an absolute need to have their own physical sexual desires fulfilled. Typically this can be rectified by communicating with a dominant partner who can then help with the submissive's longings.

sub drop
The term for feelings of fatigue, guilt, or depression that can come from prolonged sessions of submission. Sub drop can be treated by offering post-session aftercare (see page 10) and constantly communicating about the submissive's needs.

sucking face
A slang term for kissing.

sucking off
A slang term for oral sex, particularly fellatio.

sumata
A partnered masturbatory act in which a person puts their penis between their partner's thighs and thrusts between them to masturbate.

suplex
An oral sex position where the giving partner sits on the edge of a low bed or chair, and the receiving partner lies down in front of them, placing their buttocks on the giver's lap and spreading their legs. The giving partner can then initiate oral sex while remaining seated.

surf's up
Sex in the doggy style position on a surfboard while on the water. Only recommended when the water is calm, so there's no chance of being flipped off the board.

suspension bar
A metal bar attached to a wall or ceiling that can hold a sex swing or other suspension restraints.

suspension frame
A freestanding metal frame of any shape that is used to bind someone or restrain them by tying them to the frame. Also known as a suspension rack.

swing club/swing party
A social club or event where swingers will meet to switch partners or participate in swinging orgies.

swinging
A sexual lifestyle in which a married couple or a romantically committed couple will have sexual relationships with other married or committed couples, or swap partners. Jealousy is not a factor in most swinging relationships, since many swingers experience candaulism (see page 36) or have a cuckold fetish (see cuckold, page 46).

switch
In the BDSM community, a person who can participate in sessions as either a dominant or submissive partner.

swolly
A person who participates in both swinging and poly-

amory. Such people enjoy multiple romantic and sexual relationships, as well as casual sex and one-night stands.

Sybian
A vibrating sex toy that is shaped like a saddle and can be mounted for stimulation.

symphorphilia
A fetish for witnessing or experiencing a disaster, either natural ones (such as floods or wildfires) or man-made disasters such as bomb blasts. (Also see apocalypse sex, page 21).

T

tack bra
A piece of BDSM clothing; a bra with a space for inserts, which include small tacks that poke out from the fabric. The inserts can face towards the wearer (if the wearer is a submissive) or away from the wearer (if the wearer is a dominant).

Takate Kote
A common type of rope bondage that binds the arms to the torso.

tamakeri
A sex act similar to ball-busting (see page 26), in which a partner will hit or punch another partner's testicles when they are close to climax or in the midst of an orgasm.

tantalolagnia
A fetish for the feeling of sexual arousal that is caused by being teased, either verbally or physically.

Tantra
A sexual belief system in which the emotional and spiritual connection of sex is given priority over the physical feelings; practitioners of Tantric sex believe that a better spiritual connection with a partner leads to a more fulfilling physical relationship.

tape gag
An adhesive strip that is placed over a submissive's mouth to prevent speech and restrict mouth movement.

taphephilia
A fetish for the thought or act of being buried alive in sand, concrete, or other materials.

teabagging
A sex act where a person with testicles repeatedly slaps them against a sexual partner's face or puts them in a partner's mouth. This can be used as an act of dominance or as foreplay for oral sex.

teasing
The act of sexually stimulating someone without giving them a climax or orgasm. This differs from orgasm denial

(see page 108), since teasing is typically done to heighten an eventual orgasm or done in a way to ensure maximum sexual readiness.

technophilia
An intense sexual attraction to electronics, including computers, cell phones, robots, and anything that operates with electricity. Technophiles will often incorporate electronics into their sexual activity.

technosexual
Someone who is solely attracted to electronic items and has no wish to pursue sexual relationships with humans.

teddy
A type of lingerie; a very short dress made of either lace or transparent cloth, designed to make the wearer look mysterious or ethereal.

teledildonics
A general term for sex toys that are operated electronically, particularly those that are used in conjunction with video or voice chat services. There are dildos and fleshlights that can be wirelessly connected to one another, so that two people can "feel" each other remotely while having sex. The technology for this is fairly new and still being enhanced, but it's estimated that within the next

fifty years, people will be able to have physical sex with each other from opposite ends of the globe.

telephonicophilia
The fetish or sexual preference for phone sex (see page 121).

temperature play
A sexual technique that involves the placement of hot or cold items on the body to elicit new or shocking sexual sensations. Using ice cubes on the body is a good example of temperature play.

tentacle fetish
A sexual fascination with tentacles and creatures with tentacles, such as octopuses. People with this fetish enjoy seeing people penetrated by tentacles—typically in drawings or animation.

tenting
1. A term for the arousal of a person with a vagina, where the vaginal walls will extend and the clitoris will become engorged.

2. A slang term for an erection.

teratophilia
An intense sexual fascination with monsters or inhuman

creatures. Those with teratophilia, which is also known as a monster fetish, engage in fantasies of being dominated or controlled by these creatures and enjoy the exclusivity of being with a rare type of living thing.

tertiary relationship
The bottom placement in a polyamorous relationship. People who are considered tertiary are given the lowest priority and lowest amount of time in a polyamorous person's life.

testicle cuffs
BDSM restraints which are meant to be worn around the testicles. Shaped like metal rings, the cuffs wrap around the top of the scrotum, preventing the testicles from moving.

testicles
The sexual organ that produces the sperm that is released into semen. Some people view testicles as sexual in their own right, but more often they are grouped together with the penis in the sexual gaze.

thermoplastic elastomer
A common material for sex toys. Thermoplastic elastomer, sometimes abbreviated as TPE, has the advantage of being moldable into any shape, but when a cured product is stretched or manipulated, it will always return to its molded shape. It is considered one of the best body-safe

materials, as it is nonporous, latex free (for those with allergies), and does not use phthalates.

thesauromania
A fetish for women's clothing—including all items of clothing, not just underclothing or lingerie. People with this fetish tend to focus on the clothes belonging to a specific woman, making it more about a person than about the items of clothing, but will still want to masturbate or perform sexual acts with those clothing items.

thigh fetish
A fetish for thighs, including the desire to penetrate thighs or rub against thighs.

threesome
Any sexual activity or session that involves three people.

throat swab position
An oral sex position where the giving partner lies on a couch or bed with their head slightly elevated and is penetrated orally by a partner who is kneeling or standing above them.

throne job
A masturbatory sex act where masturbation takes place while seated on a chair or couch, typically while watching pornography or a live sexual act.

thumbcuffs
A BDSM sex toy consisting of metal rings joined together by a chain that are designed to lock around the thumbs, making it difficult for a submissive to hold their hands far apart.

tickler
A sex toy; a long, thin rod with feathers attached to the end of it, meant for lightly stimulating the body through tickling.

tie and tease
A BDSM sex act in which a bound person is brought to the brink of climax, only to be edged for a prolonged period of time.

time limit
The predetermined length of time that a single BDSM scene can last. For example, a submissive may know they are only able to handle three hours of a single sexual experience before they will get tired.

timophilia
A fetish for gold or physical wealth, like cash or jewelry.

tittyfucking
The sexual act of rubbing a penis or other body part or object between a partner's breasts for stimulation.

to completion
The phrase used to describe any sex act in which a partner experiences climax or orgasm. For example, "tittyfucking someone to completion" means masturbating a partner between a pair of breasts until they orgasm.

tongue punch
A slang term for oral sex in which the tongue is used for a vast majority of the act.

tonsil exam
A slang term for oral sex.

TOCOTOX
An acronym for "too complicated to explain," a term used by those in polyamorous, swinging, and other relationships with many people when talking about their sexual status.

top
1. A slang term for a giving partner during penetrative sex.

2. A slang term for the dominant partner in a BDSM relationship.

topping
Taking on a dominant role during sexual activities. This can be done by anyone, not necessarily someone who is typically dominant.

total denial
A term for the use of barriers such as chastity belts or cock cages to prevent all genital contact. This is a form of orgasm control (see page 107).

train position
A group sex position in which all participants are connected to each other in a trainlike manner, each person penetrating the person in front of them.

trainer
A dominant person in a BDSM community who is responsible for showing new people how to correctly participate in BDSM activities.

training collar
A collar worn by a submissive to signify that they are in the beginning stages of a more permanent arrangement with their dominant partner. This is seen as being almost like an engagement ring in the BDSM community.

trampling
A sex act in which one partner walks on the body of another partner to incite sexual arousal or stimulation.

transformation fetish
A sexual fascination with the thought of humans transforming into animals or inanimate objects. Often this

arousal comes from the thought of oneself transforming into a preferred object.

transvestophilia
A fetish for crossdressing (wearing the clothes of the opposite gender) or for seeing someone else crossdress. Also known as a transvestic fetish.

trick
A slang term for a person who purchases the service of a sex worker.

triple penetration
A sex act in which a person is penetrated in the mouth, vagina, and anus at the same time by three different partners.

tripsolagnophilia
A fetish for massages; someone with this fetish cannot help becoming sexually aroused when being massaged or touched in a nonsexual way.

trisexual
A person who is open to trying any kind of sexual activity. Also called a trysexual.

trouple
A committed romantic or sexual relationship involving three people instead of the typical two.

turning tricks
A slang term for having sex with clients in exchange for money.

turtle position
A variation on doggy style, this penetrative sex position has the receiving partner on all fours; they then lean back and drop so that their abdomen is on their knees and their chest is on the floor. The giving partner can then penetrate the receiving partner from behind.

twat
A slang term for the vulva.

twink
A slang term for a young and attractive gay man.

two-column tie
Any bondage act that binds two body parts together.

U

Ugol's Law
A term in sexual culture that states you are never alone in your kink; if you fetishize something, there is more than likely someone else in the world who shares your fetish.

> There are many statements of sexual logic that have become cultural "laws" or "rules" within sex communities. Similar to Ugol's Law is the slang term Rule 34, which states that if it exists in life, there is a pornographic rendition of it somewhere (usually on the Internet).

Ultra Realistic 3.0
A type of thermoplastic elastomer made from a mix of PVC and silicone, which is used to make ultra-realistic sex toys. This type of material is great for molding detailed toys.

unbirthing
A sexual fantasy about crawling back into a vagina and experiencing the cycle of birth in reverse.

unbutton the mutton
A slang term for taking a penis out of one's pants.

uncut
The term for an uncircumcised penis, which some people prefer. (See acucullophilia, page 8).

under the cuckoo's nest position
An oral sex position in which the receiving partner stands and places one leg up on a chair or other surface. The giving partner can then position themself underneath the receiving partner's groin and initiate oral sex.

under the sink position
A cunnilingus position in which the giving partner lies faceup on a bed or other raised surface, then hangs their head slightly off of the edge. The receiving partner then straddles the giving partner's head while standing, allowing them to touch the giving partner's body while getting oral sex.

unicorn
A slang term for a person in the polyamory or swinging community who will have sex with partners of any gender or sexuality, particularly with both a husband and wife in

a heterosexual swinging relationship. Unicorns tend to be bisexual or pansexual.

uniform play
The incorporation of uniforms (such as cop uniforms, nurse outfits, chef aprons and hats, etc.) into sexual role-playing.

up the middle position
An analingus position in which both partners are down on all fours, with the giving partner facing the buttocks of the receiving partner. The receiving partner's legs should be spread out a little wider than the giving partner's.

urethra
The tube that carries urine and ejaculatory fluids out of the body.

urethra play
Sex acts in which tubes or other items are inserted into the urethra for sexual stimulation.

urophilia
A fetish for urine, including smelling urine, urinating, watching someone urinate, or being urinated on.

ursusagalmatophilia
A fetish for teddy bears. Ursusagalmatophilia is a type of plushophilia (see page 128).

urtication

A BDSM sex act where a dominant partner will rub a submissive's skin with nettles, causing hives to develop on contact sites.

*Note: if practicing urtication, it is recommended that you or your partner keep an antihistamine nearby in case of a severe allergic reaction.

uteromania

A technical term for an obsession with sex in those with vaginas and uteruses. (Also see hypersexuality, page 81).

uterus

The reproductive organ that houses a growing fetus when a person is pregnant.

V

vacuum bed
A BDSM mummification device consisting of two sheets of latex; a submissive person lies between them, and the air is then vacuumed out, trapping the person inside. The trapped person breathes through a tiny tube.

vagina
A sexual and reproductive organ which extends into the body. The vagina is one part of the vulva, which is the sexual/reproductive system typically found in females.

vagina extender
A vaginal penetration sex act where a person will form an O shape with their hand at the opening of their vagina, giving extra tight stimulation to a partner who is penetrating them.

vaginal dilator
A sex toy that is used to stretch the inner walls of the vaginal canal, making it more amenable to penetration with thicker objects.

vaginal hook
A BDSM sex toy; a metal or plastic hook that is inserted into the vagina.

vaginal steam bath
A treatment where a person with a vagina sits over a bowl of steam infused with several different herbs. This is said to help with vaginal soreness from sex or to stimulate more intense vaginal arousal.

vaginismus
A medical condition in which any penetration of the vagina, sexual or not, causes immense pain.

vagitarian
A slang term for a person who fetishizes cunnilingus.

vajankle
A sex toy that is shaped like a foot with an opening (which resembles a vaginal opening) at the top of where the ankle would be. This allows people with a foot fetish to have sex with a foot.

vampire gloves

A BDSM clothing item consisting of gloves with spikes attached to the fingers and palms, meant to pierce or lightly scratch a submissive's skin.

vampirism

A fetish for vampires or vampiric culture, including dark, gothic clothing; blood play (see page 31); biting fetishes; and/or sadomasochism.

vanilla

A person (typically heterosexual) who prefers basic sexual intercourse within a committed romantic relationship. Vanilla people have no interest in "unusual" sexualities or kinky behavior.

vanilla audience

A type of BDSM humiliation where a submissive will be required to perform sexual acts in front of an audience comprised of vanilla people, causing the audience to verbalize their disgust.

vee

A polyamorous relationship involving exactly three people, where two partners will each have sex with the third partner, but not with each other.

veil fetish
A fetish for wearing a veil or for seeing a partner wear a veil.

velvet fetish
A fetish for clothes, items, and sexual objects made of velvet.

venereal disease
Another name for an STI (see page 194).

venus butterfly position
A mutual masturbation position in which both partners are seated on the ground, legs spread and facing each other. They move closely together so that the tips of their genitals are touching, then gently rub them together in order to masturbate them. This position is unlikely to allow either partner to achieve orgasm, but it's a great foreplay act.

Viagra
The most common medical fix for erectile dysfunction; a pill that artificially directs blood flow to the penis in order to cause an erection.

vibrators
A type of sex toy that emits a range of mild to intense vibrations meant to stimulate sexual organs.

vicarphilia

The fetish for hearing about other people's sexual adventures, or hearing someone describe what they are doing to themself sexually. Many phone sex workers cater specifically to vicarphiliacs.

vincilagnia

A fetish for bondage, including BDSM acts.

violet wand

A sex toy that channels electricity through a long wand; when touched, it gives a very soft electric shock to the user. This is a great toy for electrophiliacs (see electrophilia, page 56).

virgin

The term for someone who has never had a specific type of intercourse before. The term generally refers to someone who has never had vaginal intercourse, but it can be applied to any sexual act—for example, someone who has never had oral sex before is an oral virgin.

virgin fetish

The term for someone who has an intense attraction to those who are virgins.

virtual sex

Any sexual activity that utilizes virtual communication

devices, such as web cameras, phones, or messaging programs. Virtual sex takes place in digital spaces, which can be great for technophiles (see technophilia, page 202) or those in long-distance relationships.

vominatrix
A ProDomme or dominatrix who specializes in making clients vomit.

vorarephilia
A sexual fascination with the thought of being eaten by another person or of eating one's partner.

voyeurism
A fetish for watching other people performing sex acts, with or without the permission of those being watched. Someone with this fetish is known as a voyeur.

vulva
The collective term for the inner labia, outer labia, clitoris, and vaginal opening.

W

walk of shame

The term for the return home (via walking or public transportation) after a one-night stand or a night of anonymous sex. Those doing a walk of shame typically wear the same clothes they had on the day before and have a disheveled look.

For many, the walk of shame has always been seen as a sad thing, a sign of a night of sexual passion gone wrong, but history tells of a walk of shame that stemmed from a sexual love that seemed very right. While today's walk of shame is self-inflicted, this historical walk of shame (called a penance walk) was punishment for sexual immorality sent down by King Richard III upon Jane Shore. Jane was King Henry IV's most beloved mistress; she seemed to be a kind soul who never used her favor with the King for personal gain. By all accounts, she loved the King deeply, and he loved her. When he died suddenly, Jane helped settle a long-standing feud between King Henry's widow, Elizabeth Woodville, and William Hastings, his chamberlain. Her help allowed Elizabeth and King Henry's son, Edward V, to claim the throne. When Edward disappeared less than a year after his father's death, Richard was crowned king. Richard was not too thrilled with Jane's involvement in the fight to keep King Henry's son on the throne, and accused her of using her sexuality to inspire conspiratorial behavior. Jane's punishment was to walk through the streets of London wearing (according to most historians) nothing but a thin sheet, while onlookers shouted obscenities and threw dirt and rocks at her. (If this sounds familiar to you, yes, it was the inspiration for the famous walk of atonement scene from *A Song of Ice and Fire*).

---

wang

A slang term for a penis.

wanking

A slang term for masturbating, especially masturbating a penis.

Wartenberg wheel

A BDSM device designed to cause sharp pain on a submissive's skin. Shaped like a pizza cutter, but with spikes around the edge of the wheel, the device is rolled up and down a person's body, piercing the skin and causing marks.

water bondage

The term for restraining someone underwater for sex play.

*Note: extended use of water bondage could cause the partner being held under the water to drown. If practicing water bondage, it is recommended to limit each instance of the act to very short periods of time.

water-based lubricant

The most widely used type of lubricant, this lube can be used on anything—sex toys, skin, condoms, etc. The only downside is that, being made up of mostly water, the lubricant tends to evaporate or dissolve into the skin rather easily. Several applications may be needed for a single sex session.

waterfall position

A penetrative sex position that is a variation of the cowgirl position. The giving partner lies on their back on a raised platform, but with their head hanging off the edge of the bed. The receiving partner can then initiate penetration by straddling the giver's groin.

wax play

The act of sensually dripping hot wax onto a partner's skin as a form of temperature play (see page 203). There are candles that are made specifically for wax play that don't allow the wax to get too hot; the goal is not to burn anyone, just to give an exciting feeling.

well-endowed
An adjective that describes people who have larger-than-average sex organs.

wet clothes fetish
A fetish for seeing a partner wearing wet clothing, or for getting wet while wearing clothing.

wet dreams
Orgasms that happen randomly while one is sleeping, often brought on by sexual dreams. Unlike with sleep masturbation (see page 183), the sleeping person does not touch themselves to trigger orgasm—the orgasm happens without physical stimulation.

wet ride
A sex session in the cowgirl or reverse cowgirl position that takes place in a tub or swimming pool.

whacking off
A slang term for masturbating a penis.

wheelbarrow position
A penetrative sex position where the receiving partner goes into a push-up position on the ground; the giving partner stands behind them. The giving partner picks up the ankles and legs of the receiver and holds them while penetrating their partner.

whip
A long, thin, leather sex toy that is used in BDSM to inflict a stinging pain on a submissive.

whipping post
A freestanding and sturdy structure to which a submissive partner can be bound for prolonged bouts of whipping.

whiskey dick
The slang term for when a penis cannot become erect due to a high blood alcohol level.

woody
A slang term for an erection.

working girl
A euphemistic term for a female sex worker.

worship
The term for fetishizing a particular part of the body. For example, someone who practices hand worship loves hands and wants to lavish a partner's hands with affection.

wrist cuffs
A BDSM sex toy consisting of bands of metal, plastic, or leather that are connected by a chain. The bands are put over a partner's wrists to keep the arms close together and limit arm movement.

X

X-rated

The term for any media which includes sexually explicit content, such as pornography or erotica.

Everyone knows that X means FOR ADULT EYES ONLY. But just how did the letter X come to be associated with adult content? It actually started because of a copyright issue: when the movie rating system (designed by the Motion Picture Association of America so that movie-goers would know which films were suitable for a family audience) went into effect in 1968, filmmakers could self-apply the ratings if they thought their films were too racy to be seen by children. An X-rating was meant to connote sexual implication and crude language. However, since the MPAA did not copyright the ratings system, producers releasing fully pornographic movies were also free to use the ratings for their movies, which actually helped bring pornos more into the spotlight for the everyday consumer. Porn distribution centers even started competing with each other, adding multiple X's to the covers of their films to show that their movies were hotter than the others. Not wanting feature films to be associated with "dirty films," the MPAA eventually changed their own X-rating to the NC-17 rating, leaving X squarely in the realm of porn.

xenophilia

An intense sexual attraction to strangers or foreigners. This also describes a fetish for extraterrestrial life, a.k.a. aliens.

Y

yaoi
A sexual culture centered around the romantic and sexual love between males. Participants in yaoi culture love media about gay relationships, erotic stories of physical male love, and watching male partners have sex.

Yaoi may be the main name of the male-male love culture, but the word is actually an acronym for the Japanese phrase *yama nashi, ochi nashi, imi nashi,* translated to no climax, *no point, and no meaning.* However, the phrase isn't referencing the sexuality displayed by yaoi characters; it represents the flow of the stories that feature yaoi characters, which tend to focus on the emotional component of the male-male relationship rather than any story plot points.

yeastiality

A sexual fetish for bread, dough, or pastries. This can include eating dough items while having sex, physically having sex with a bread item (such as a doughnut or bagel), or smelling yeast.

yiffing

The term for sex acts between two or more people in the furry community. Yiffing typically happens while in costume or fursuits.

YKINMK

An acronym for "your kink is not my kink," a term used in the kink and BDSM community to express respect for someone else's fetish while also acknowledging that it is not something one personally enjoys.

YKINOK

An acronym for "your kink is not okay"; this typically is used in reference to nonconsensual or illegal activities.

yoni egg

A type of sex toy or vaginal exerciser that is inserted into the vagina to help strengthen vaginal muscles.

Z

Z-job
An act of oral sex that takes place while the receiving partner is sleeping. Often this will be done to wake up a sleeping person, so that they begin receiving pleasure immediately upon waking.

*Note: if you want to try a Z-job with your partner, make sure you receive consent the night before or sometime prior to when you want to preform the act so it's not a complete surprise.

zelophilia
A fetish for feelings of extreme jealousy.

zipper dinner
A slang term for fellatio; also referred to as "zipper sex."

zoophilia
A fetish for animals, including looking at animals or

fantasizing about animals. Zoophilia does not necessarily include acts of bestiality (see page 233), since it focuses more on the thought of human/animal intercourse than the actual act. Those who experience zoophilia are called zoosexuals.

Nonconsensual terms

acquaintance rape
The general term for rape (see page 235) that occurs between people who know each other.

avisodomy
A variation of bestiality (see following definition) specific to birds.

bestiality
The term for any sex act involving a human and an animal. Though the animal may "participate" by exhibiting sexual behavior, it still cannot give true consent, and this is considered a nonconsensual act.

biastophilia
A fetish for assaulting people, typically strangers. Biastophilia is often considered to be a type of extreme sadism.

death fantasy
A fetish for the idea of death in general, or for the idea of killing one's partner during sex.

dippoldism
A fetish for spanking, hitting, or applying other physical punishment to children.

erotophonophilia
A fetish for committing murder or for seeing someone be murdered.

frotteurism
A fetish for rubbing one's body or genitals on nonconsenting people. This typically happens in a crowded public area, like a train or elevator.

necrophilia
A fetish for corpses, including sexual activity with dead bodies.

ophidicism
The act of inserting the tail of a reptile (particularly a snake or lizard) into the vagina or anus. This is a form of bestiality.

parthenophagy
A fetish for the idea or practice in eating young women,

particularly those that are virgins. This is a type of voraphilia.

pedophilia
A sexual disorder that causes someone to be attracted to very young children, typically age thirteen and younger. A person who performs any sexual activity on a child is called a pedophile.

peodeiktophilia
A fetish for exposing one's penis to a non-consenting individual, either through public flashing, photo, or video.

piquerism
A fetish for piercing another person's skin without consent. Piercing is usually done with objects such as knives or pins, and the acts are centered on erogenous zones, such as the breast or groin area.

public exposure
The deliberate exposure of one's naked body—specifically the genitals, breasts, or buttocks—in public. Also known as flashing.

rape
A form of sexual assault in which one or more persons will use force or threats to have sexual intercourse with someone against their will and without their consent. Rape is an illegal activity and punishable by law.

rape fantasy

A fantasy about raping someone. Having rape fantasies does not necessarily mean that a person will rape in real life; there are many men and women who fantasize about rape or being raped who would not act on these fantasies. Many of these people are turned on by the thought of being in control or of relinquishing control to someone. While having a rape fantasy is not a nonconsensual act, because it involves thoughts of nonconsensual activities, it is included in this section.

raptophilia

A fetish state in which arousal is dependent upon sexually assaulting someone, including molesting or raping someone.

revenge porn

Any media, including photographic images or video, which includes nude or explicit images of a person who has not consented to be in them or has not consented to have the videos distributed to the public. These photos or videos are typically distributed to wide audiences online to cause intense humiliation to the person in them. Unfortunately, revenge porn is commonly made or distributed by ex-partners of the person in the photos or videos as an act of "revenge" for relationship issues. Distribution of revenge porn is illegal and is punishable by law.

sexual abuse/sexual assault
Any unwanted sexual activity that comes about through threat or force. Also known as molestation.

snuff porn/snuff films
A genre of pornography that shows a person, typically female, who is raped and then murdered. There are faux snuff films where the porn actresses only pretend to be murdered, but these are still viewed as highly immoral videos. Snuff films are illegal and making a snuff film is punishable by law.

somnophilia
A sexual fascination for having sex with someone who is sleeping, with or without consent.

statutory rape
Any sex act involving a minor or a person suffering from debilitating mental illness. Such people are unable to truly consent to sexual activity.

stranger rape
The term for any act of rape or sexual assault where the perpetrator and the victim do not know each other.

ACKNOWLEDGEMENTS

The Sextionary would not have been possible without the help of Jason Ryan Strawsburg and Kurt Heinrich, who worked tirelessly to research every single term in this book, and Cleis Press editor Stephanie Lippitt who wrote all of the definitions and essays. Many thanks to them for creating this wonderful resource for the sexually curious!